A Hitler Youth in Poland

▼

Jost Hermand

A HITLER YOUTH IN POLAND

The Nazis' Program for Evacuating Children during World War II

Translated by Margot Bettauer Dembo

NORTHWESTERN UNIVERSITY PRESS
EVANSTON, ILLINOIS

Northwestern University Press
Evanston, Illinois 60208-4210

Originally published in German under the title *Als Pimpf in Polen: Erweiterte Kinderlandverschickung, 1940–1945*. Copyright © 1993 by Fischer Taschenbuch Verlag, GmbH, Frankfurt am Main. English translation copyright © 1997 by Northwestern University Press. Published 1997. All rights reserved.

Printed in the United States of America

10 9 8 7 6 5 4 3 2

ISBN 0-8101-1291-4 (cloth)
ISBN 0-8101-1292-2 (paper)

Library of Congress Cataloging-in-Publication Data

Hermand, Jost.
   [Als Pimpf in Poland. English]
   A Hitler Youth in Poland: the Nazis' program for evacuating children during World War II / Jost Hermand; translated by Margot Bettauer Dembo.
     p. cm.
   ISBN 0-8101-1291-4 (cloth : alk. paper). — ISBN 0-8101-1292-2 (pbk. : alk. paper)
    1. Hermand, Jost. 2. Hitler-Jugend — Biography. 3. Kinderlandverschickung (Organization : Germany) 4. World War, 1939–1945 — Children — Germany. 5. World War, 1939–1945 — Personal narratives, German. 6. Poland — History — Occupation, 1939–1945. I. Dembo, Margot Bettauer. II. Title.
DD253.5.H4613 1997
943.086'083 — dc21
                                97-39746
                                 CIP

The paper used in this publication meets the minimum requirements of the American National Standard for Information Sciences — Permanence of Paper for Printed Library Materials, ANSI Z39.48-1984.

To the memory of my mother, Annelies Hermand (1907–59)

CONTENTS

▼

INTRODUCTION
The Difficulties of Reappraising a Traumatic Experience

▼

The National Socialist educational system has been under
scrutiny for more than four decades. One would think that
even the darkest aspects of this phenomenon, so crucial to
an understanding of German fascism, have by now been
explored. But this is not the case. Certainly there are com-
pilations of documents and accounts that deal in a general
way with the Nazi educational system, as well as specifically with the Adolf Hitler Schools, the National Political
Institutes of Education (*Napolas*), and the *Ordensburgen*,
where the young elite of the new Reich were to have been
trained and educated,[1] but there is almost no comparable
documentation for the everyday fascist routine and ap-
proaches to teaching at the countless public elementary,
junior high, and senior high schools of the Third Reich.[2]
Consequently, we know little about how indoctrination was
pursued in these institutions, the ranking of students based
on performance, their anxieties, or even to what extent idealistic enthusiasm may have prevailed in the schools.

Indeed, one form of educational training has received
only marginal attention so far, namely, the *Kinderlandverschickung* (KLV), the Nazis' evacuation of children from
the larger cities to rural areas. Tens of thousands, if not
hundreds of thousands,[3] of children were affected by this
policy between 1933 and 1940; and later, when the KLV
was expanded between 1940 and 1945, more than 2.8 mil-

lion boys and girls were sent off to rural areas.[4] Many of those who had to take part as children in the KLV (referred to sarcastically as *Kinderlandverschleppung*)—those born between 1927 and 1934 who lived in big cities threatened by Allied air raids—consider it a relic of their past. They speak of it only reluctantly and usually only with other KLV participants. And so, because of the silence of this older generation,[5] Germans who were born after 1934 either know nothing about the KLV experience or they think of it as unimportant because they have rarely heard or read about it.

As a result of this widespread repression, we are faced with the singular fact that one of the largest population movements of the twentieth century has left lasting effects only in the conscious or subconscious of those who were evacuated. From October 1940 on, more than two million children and young people were forced, often from one day to the next, to leave their homes and parents. They were taken to distant rural areas, as far away as Denmark, Latvia, Croatia, Hungary, Bulgaria, Slovakia, and occupied Poland.

Obviously, any mention of this exodus in the public press after 1945 was taboo. Nor is there any reference to the KLV camps in East or West German literature,[6] even though the examination of childhood under fascism has been one of the chief themes of writers in both these literatures ever since the publication of works like Günter Grass's *Die Blechtrommel* (*The Tin Drum*) (1959) and *Katz und Maus* (*Cat and Mouse*) (1961), and Christa Wolf's *Kindheitsmuster* (*A Model Childhood*) (1976).[7] Moreover, the "Expanded Evacuation of Children" has been largely ignored up to now by German historians, sociologists, pedagogues, and literary scholars, although over the past twenty years they have tackled almost every other sociohistorical problem related to fascism.

There are several short essays and two books on the

subject that I should mention here. Three of these interpret the KLV experience from the viewpoint of former Nazis who had leading roles in organizing and executing this gigantic undertaking. Clearly their primary strategy is to justify themselves, to show their involvement in fascism as well-intentioned, if not heroic. Probably the most brazen of this group is Otto Würschinger, who proudly introduces himself as "Combat Commander of the Hitler Youth Reich Leadership [*Reichführung*] during the final battle for Berlin." In his 1979 treatise about the KLV, he calls the role the Hitler Youth (*Hitler Jugend*) performed in giving "extracurricular care" to the youths in the KLV camps "an integral ongoing part of German national history" because of the supposedly high ideals and the comradeship practiced by all, of which, he adds, no one could have any doubts.[8] Würschinger even claims that the "war generation" and the "Hitler Youth generation" who grew up in the "volkish cult of the Third Reich" would under no circumstances have "capitulated" at the end of the war because of the proud and self-confident attitude instilled in them by the "Hitler Youth leaders, both male and female," who were inspired by their unswerving love for Germany. "On the contrary," he writes, "the German Federal Republic's reconstruction, its economic miracle, and its position as a world power are their work."[9]

Jutta Rüdiger, former "official adviser to the Reich Leader [*Reichsführer*] of the League of German Girls [*Bund Deutscher Mädel*]," was just as enthusiastic in her 1983 book about the National Socialist decision to evacuate children to the country.[10] Like Würschinger, Rüdiger extolls the lofty ideals and the selfless team spirit that swept along all those who participated in the KLV project. This Nazi Party operation was a "unique achievement," she writes; indeed it was "the greatest *social accomplishment* in behalf of youth in our history." There was no "hard work and no corporal punishment" in the KLV camps, nor were "young people belittled in the eyes of others, their sense of self-respect was not offended, there were no punishment drills or punitive reductions in food rations." From the outset the camps were supposedly characterized by "decent behavior, upright character, and patriotic devotion"—all virtues that are scarcely imaginable in quite this same form today.[11]

Both Otto Würschinger's and Jutta Rüdiger's essays are based on statistics, historical cross-references, and other factual details from the archive of the *Arbeitsgemeinschaft KLV* (KLV Study Group), which was still in existence at the time they were writing. Some of these archival materials were published by Gerhard Dabel, the first chairman of the archive, in his 1981 book *KLV: Die Erweiterte Kinderlandverschickung*. The same fascist euphemisms if not outright glorification of the KLV experience underlie his book and the two above-mentioned articles. Dabel was a former Hitler Youth leader, the author of Nazi literature for young people, and the last director of the KLV Headquarters in the Reich Youth Leadership. In the early forties he published a series of patently Nazi novels for young readers.[12] Indeed, Dabel reveals his sympathy for the Nazi regime by proudly pointing out that Ernst Dombrowski, one of the leading National Socialist graphic artists, made several woodcuts available for Dabel's KLV volume.[13] These, he claimed, were comparable to the works of Albrecht Dürer and Ludwig Richter.[14] Dabel's book is almost uniformly enthusiastic and approving; it suggests that in setting up the KLV camps those in charge within the National Socialist German Workers Party (the Nazi Party), even Hitler himself, were concerned only with making sure, on humanitarian grounds, that "innocent" German youth be protected from the "evil" air raids by the British and later the Americans, giving young people the chance to live in the safety of a rural setting.[15] The KLV emerges from this collection of documents as a kind of *Kraft durch Freude* (Strength-through-Joy) movement expanded to include young people. In Dabel's view, it became the "most beautiful," or at least "the most important," experience in the lives of the evacuated children—despite the separation from their parents.[16]

The other book about the 1940-45 evacuation of children is also based on Dabel's collection of documents, but *Der Zug der Kinder* (The procession of the children) by Claus Larass takes a more journalistic approach. At the very beginning of his book, Larass specifically thanks the Freiburg KLV Study Group and its chairman, Gerhard Dabel, without whose active help, he acknowledges, the book never would have come into being. In addition, the author includes in his reports on the camps short sketches about the KLV experiences written by Loki Schmidt, Ralf Dahrendorf, and Jürgen Roland—former KLV teachers and students. In contrast to Dabel, Larass also points out several negative aspects of life in the camps, such as homesickness that diminished only gradually, the constant fear the weaker children felt of those who were stronger, and widespread bedwetting. But despite these reservations, his overview is just as positive.[17] He praises "the camaraderie, the life on the land, gratification of the longing for adventure, and the young people's feeling that they were being taken seriously." He writes that in these camps there was neither the prominent brutality promoted by some National Socialist theorists nor the overemphasis on sex so prevalent today. True, there were "affairs and entanglements," but "most of these flirtations" remained in the realm of "tender innocence." The teachers in particular, even though they were separated from their wives, showed an "uncommonly high degree of responsible behavior" under the "extraordinary conditions" of life in the camps. As a result, for many of the children the KLV was, in the end, a "beautiful" experience—despite separation from their parents, "repressed anxiety," and the National Socialist intention to train them as "willing tools of the new rulers."[18]

It is outrageous that statements of this sort should not have been challenged before now. Why do those who participated in the KLV remain silent in the face of such perversions of the truth? Were their experiences in these camps really as innocuous, or even beneficial, as Würschinger, Rüdiger, Dabel, and Larass want us to believe? Weren't many of the children and young people in these camps made to feel inferior and weren't they forced to endure constant harassment and drilling, the worst kind of cruelty, endless cross-country marches, arduous paramilitary exercises, and gross attempts at indoctrination—leading to the sort of gang brutalization depicted in William Golding's *Lord of the Flies* (1954)? And was it really only the weaker boys who were driven to the edge by the collective drill? In camps where, instead of teachers, Hitler Youth squad leaders (*Lagermannschaftsführer* or *Lamafüs*) were in charge, wasn't it inevitable that all inmates were subjected to the fanaticism and sadistic excesses that defined the National Socialist hierarchy as a whole?

It isn't easy to answer questions like these with a clear yes or no. Indeed, it's almost impossible to make any generalizations on this subject. There probably were KLV camps like the ones Dabel and Larass describe. Why couldn't there have been cases of individualized care, of comradely experiences in the KLV? After all, even in prisons, concentration camps, army barracks, and severely regimented boarding schools, feelings of humanity can't be completely suppressed. But KLV camps in which the caring element predominated were surely not the educational institutions that the fanatics in the Nazi leadership groups envisioned. These men, who were committed to war and victory, were not concerned with educational methods that—as a mark of true humanity—would offer all children, including the retarded or handicapped, a chance to develop. They emphasized primarily those things that would prepare young people for later duties in the service of

National Socialism. Their objective, translated into the language of the Hitler Youth, still reverberates in my mind because it was repeated so often. It goes something like this: "The German youth must be slender and supple, fast as a greyhound, tough as leather, and hard as Krupp steel. He must learn to do without, to endure criticism and injustice, to be reliable, discreet, decent, and loyal."[19]

Adolf Hitler had described this educational system in great detail in *Mein Kampf* (1925–27).[20] Subsequently, on many different occasions, he added specific details and supplemented and refined his original ideas, culminating in his *Monologe im Führerhauptquartier* (Monologues in the Führer's headquarters) (1941–42).[21] The system would focus on toughening up youths, on political instruction, and on selection of the fittest. The idea was to reduce to a minimum residual liberal impulses like self-realization, forging German youth into a so-called Nordic—but in reality an unprincipled—body of followers who would blindly obey any order from above, as expressed in the maxim "You are nothing—your Volk is everything!" Therefore, "education" for young males, who were Hitler's primary concern, meant mainly what many National Socialists accurately described as *Menschenformung*—the shaping of human beings. Girls and young women, in contrast, were primarily expected to work on the land and eventually to become mothers.[22] Consequently, Hitler approved all measures that would substitute a leader-follower principle for the "teacher-pupil relationship." Boys, Hitler felt, were primarily breeding stock for "smart and snappy" fellows, real "tough guys," "enthusiastic fighters," "political soldiers" and future "leaders."[23] That is why Hitler valued paramilitary rigor far above the memorizing of "dead facts." In recognition of this, he had emphasized in *Mein Kampf* that "the volkish state must not adjust its educational work primarily to pumping mere knowledge into young people, but rather to raising healthy bodies." Such a state, he wrote, must assume that "a less well-educated, but physically healthy individual with a sound, firm character full of determination and willpower is more valuable to the volkish community than an intellectual weakling."[24]

Hitler thus set his hopes not upon the "spoiled young sons and young ladies of the middle class," whom he often ridiculed for their pampered "sensitivity," but upon the children of the lower classes, above all, the children of peasants and farmers, blue-collar workers, and lower-level office employees. It was they, the progeny of the old school—and not the "cretins" of the middle and upper bourgeoisie—whom Hitler intended for leading positions in the state after they had received the required training. Instead of allowing "hundreds of thousands" of talented Germans "to go to the dogs in the proletarian swamp," he explained, the volkish state had to consider its first priority: to give a helping hand to the best of the youths from the lower class—the most vigorous and most eager to get things done.[25] Only in this way could a new, more robust class replace the largely degenerate middle-class element. This new class, proud of its own will to work and determined to get things done, would disdainfully reject all things foreign, all empty humanitarian slogans and pacifist illusions, and would not hesitate to place themselves at the head of the German people, of all Europe, if not of the entire world. Expanding on this theme in the early thirties, Hitler said to Hermann Rauschning, who became the National Socialist chairman of the Danzig Senate in 1933: "My pedagogy is hard. All that is weak must be chiseled away. In my Ordensburgen a new type of youth will grow up who will shock the world. I want a brutal, domineering, fearless, and cruel youth. [My] young people must be all these things. They must endure pain. There must be nothing weak or soft about them. The free, magnificent beast of prey must once again flash from their eyes. I want my young people to be strong and beautiful. I shall have them trained in all forms of physical exercise. I want an athletic youth. This is the first and most important thing. That is how I will eradicate thousands of years of human domestication. I don't want them to have an intellectual education. Knowledge would spoil my young people. I prefer that they learn only what they pick up by following their own play instinct. But they must learn self-control. I will have them master the fear of death through the most difficult trials. That is the stage of heroic youth. Out of it will grow the stage of the free man, a human being who is the measure and the center of the world."[26]

Of course this was only one aspect of Hitler's goal for education. In the long run, such a system must not only have leaders who, steeled by difficulty, privation, and self-denial, would ascend into the ranks of "free" men, it must also have hardened subordinates, transfigured by Nazi propaganda into selfless "national comrades." These subordinates would not be routed through the leadership training of the Adolf Hitler Schools, Napolas, and Ordensburgen. Hitler said so bluntly in his notorious Reichenberg speech of 8 September 1938: "These young people will learn nothing but to think German and act German. When a boy or girl joins our organizations [the Jungvolk and Jungmädelbund] at the age of ten, it is often the first time in their lives that they get to breathe and feel fresh air; then four years later they will leave the Jungvolk and go into the Hitler Youth. We will keep them there for another four years, and then we definitely will not put them back into the hands of those who created our old class and status barriers; rather we will immediately take them into the Party or into the Labor Front, into the SA [Stormtroopers] or into the SS, into the NSKK [*Kraftfahrerkorps*, Motorcycle Corps], and so on. If they haven't turned into complete National Socialists there, then they'll go into the Labor

Service where they'll be polished for another six or seven months. Those who still harbor remnants of class consciousness or snobbishness will be taken in hand for further treatment by the Wehrmacht [the army]. And so they will never be free again for the rest of their lives!"[27]

Despite the apparent contradictions of the argument—at one point German youth is described as "free," at another "not free"—this does not mean that National Socialism was an inherently dualistic system. On the contrary; in this system even the so-called free ones, the leaders, were not really free. They constantly had to be on guard against any rivals, and again and again they had to prove that they were strong in order not to be put out of the running by others even stronger.

Since Hitler held individual human life as well as the life of entire peoples and races to be primarily a Darwinian struggle, where the stronger triumph over the weaker, he forced all those who followed him or became his subjects to recognize the principle of "biological superiority" and the "basically aristocratic laws of nature."[28] In the end, for Hitler "life" was essentially chaotic, a struggle of all against all. And only the individual who had the greater determination, the unscrupulous ability to persevere, indeed, the drive to action that Nietzsche called "the will to power," would prove himself a born leader.[29]

Hitler saw this struggle beginning as early as elementary school and continuing in an intensified form in the Jungvolk and Hitler Youth. Through struggle one person would emerge as a leader and another as a follower, but in the final analysis, all would be integrated into the same brutal system, in which there was no constitutional rule and the only valid law was "survival of the fittest." Hitler was therefore fundamentally opposed to entrusting young people only to experienced, "wise" teachers. Instead—in the spirit of the phrase he had coined, "Young people must

Adolf Hitler with a Hitler Youth (ca. 1935). From Nazi-Kitsch, *ed. Rolf Steinberg (Darmstadt: Melzer, 1975).*

educate themselves"—they were to learn in the chaos of the wolf pack that the struggle of all against all would serve to preserve and strengthen the individual as well as the German Volk. This kind of education, Hitler felt, would be less likely in conventional schools, with their middle-class humanism and "softening" educational ideals, than in the Hitler Youth–controlled camps, which emphasized the toughening-up he demanded and where the "pitiless laws of nature" prevailed.

Hitler's social Darwinistic educational ideas, based on warlike training, toughening, and conquest, were supported by Alfred Rosenberg, Bernhard Rust, Wilhelm Frick, Baldur von Schirach, Alfred Bäumler, Ernst Krieck, and Hans Schemm. After 1933 these men tried to put the entire German educational and university system under strict Nazi Party control. In addition to the introduction of specific lectures in German civilization and racial policy, they resolutely championed the expansion of physical discipline intended to harden youngsters for "service to the Volk" by "training them to be fit and ready to fight."[30] Thus, as early as 9 May 1933, at a conference of state ministers of the interior, Wilhelm Frick demanded that in the "new education" system primary attention be given to the development of "a will as strong as steel," to "educating young people to fighting fitness" in order to prepare them for the impending "fight for life."[31] Baldur von Schirach also saw the "education revolution" as primarily a confrontation between the previous overintellectualization of youth and the need to strengthen their "will to fight."[32] Hans Schemm sharply criticized the older, humanistic educational ideals and their "ridiculous pacifism," praising instead the "readiness to die" as the highest goal of the new education.[33] In *Der Nationalsozialismus als Siegfriedbewegung und Kampfbejahung* (National Socialism as a Siegfried movement and affirmation of battle) he wrote: "A human being who does not strive, who does not fight, is not human. To be human means to be a fighter. To be a German means being a fighter a hundred times over; being a National Socialist means being a fighter a thousand times over."[34]

These ideas were most forcefully shaped after the start of World War II. In the years that followed, Alfred Bäumler, a professor of political pedagogy, insisted that students must be imbued with the active heroic spirit "of a proud Germanic warrior" rather than with what he saw as a decadent "spiritualism." Like Rosenberg, he placed his hopes on "readiness for action" that would declare a war of "Nordic barbarity" against all urbanity and civilization. In order to promote this process ideologically, Bäumler supported strengthening the "German man" in his "innermost being," that is to say, in his drives and instincts. He stated that membership in an "association of men" that would be ready to fight was the only legitimate form of National Socialist education.[35] Joseph Goebbels struck an even more strident note. In 1944 he declared that all that mattered now was to forget whatever reminded one of "civilized life" and to think only about intensifying the "warlike" character without which, in his view, the "German nation could not continue to exist."[36]

Catch phrases like this resounded at all levels of the Nazi educational system between 1933 and 1945. The Nazi Party continually organized ceremonies, not only in the elite schools (that is, the Adolf Hitler Schools, Napolas, and Ordensburgen) but also in elementary and high schools. The principal themes of these assemblies were heroism and the readiness to die for "the cause." As reported in the *Deutschland Berichte*, as early as 1936 many elementary school graduation ceremonies displayed the motto: "We were born to die for Germany!"[37]

Even traditional schools made every effort to change "softie" pupils into "go-getter, daredevil" types.[38] Besides the increasing emphasis on physical training, the shipping of entire school classes to rural districts between 1933 and 1944 played an important role in this transformation process. There, in camps that had been made available by the Party, teachers who were active Party members, especially Hitler Youth leaders, provided the required training and "selection" of students. The spirit that prevailed in those camps is reflected in a song sung by the young people in a 1934 KLV transport, the last lines of which are "We are the youths of the Führer, united in his spirit. /We will fight eternally for all that is German."[39] Another one of the early KLV songs contained equally overbearing and bellicose stanzas:

> Blond and suntanned boys
> aren't meant to sit in parlors.
> Boys have to fight
> have to do daredevil deeds.
> Boys have to be in the midst of life;
> boys are proud whether big or small.
> With pipes and drums and tubas,
> this is the song of the boys.
> Boys daringly defy
> stormy winds, bad weather and rain.
> Boys are the commanding kind;
> their happy journey is like
> the flight of petrels.[40]

After 1933, pressure was put on all young people between the ages of ten and eighteen to join the Hitler Youth or the League of German Girls. These organizations tried to set themselves up, first parallel to the schools and then on a level above them, as the leading educational institutions, marked by the National Socialist will to fight. Indeed, when with the introduction of compulsory youth service (*Jugenddienstpflicht*)[41] on 1 December 1936, membership in the Hitler Youth and League of German Girls became compulsory, the Party's influence in the schools increased steadily and led to a system in which the education of young people became more and more fascistic. By 1938 the various Hitler Youth organizations already had more than 8.7 million members. In the opinion of the Nazi Party, the education of German youth was handled much too "gently" in the home and in school. It was the Party's goal to corral all ten-to-fourteen-year olds into the Jungvolk and the Jungmädelbund and all fourteen-to-eighteen-year olds into the Hitler Youth and the League of German Girls and to counter traditional education with a well-structured Party educational system. This training program would give the "new" youths the feeling that they were "victorious, superior, and successful" and at the same time, through "strenuous activities, competitions, and war games,"[42] would eliminate any sense of pity "for weaker individuals, minorities, and inferior people."[43] From early on, young males were to be trained in these organizations in "unquestioning loyalty, brutality, and toughness of viewpoint."[44] As a result, from the first years of the Third Reich, the Jungvolk and the Hitler Youth as well as the Party's KLV camps leaned toward premilitary training. This training was supposed to "steel" German youth and—as the "disciplinary code of the Hitler Youth" specifically emphasized—teach them to obey unconditionally all "orders without any ifs or buts."[45]

In time, as was repeatedly demonstrated, the Hitler Youth superseded the schools. For example, on 27 September 1940, as the British air raids on the large German cities were beginning, Hitler appointed Baldur von Schirach to take all necessary steps "in conjunction with the appropriate departments in the Party and government and, if necessary, of the Wehrmacht, to set up and carry out the KLV."[46] It is noteworthy that the appointment did not go to the National Socialist League of Teachers (*Nationalsozialistische Lehrerbund*) or the Nazis' Public Welfare System (*Nationalsozialistische Volkswohlfahrt*).[47] Schirach was the former Reichsjugendführer of the Nazi Party and had been Gauleiter of the "Ostmark" (Austria) in Vienna since 1940. In his book *Die Hitler-Jugend*, he "explained war" to "former" children, especially "mama's boys," describing the Hitler Youth–organized KLV camps as the "ideal form of boys' life." As for the deeper significance of the Hitler Youth, he wrote: "The Hitler Youth is an educational community. Whoever marches in the Hitler Youth is not just one of millions, but a soldier fighting for an idea. His value to the community is to be measured by how deeply he has grasped this idea. A working-class boy whose heart beats passionately for our Führer is therefore considerably more important to Germany than a highly educated aesthete who fights against every impulse of his weak emotions with intellectual considerations." With logical consistency, Schirach demanded in this book that education in the schools must be supplemented by Hitler Youth training. Soon, he wrote, there would be no room in the new Reich for teachers who could not summon up an interest in the extracurricular activities of the Hitler Youth. In the future young people won't need uncommitted mediators to impart knowledge, or teachers to cram things down their throats, or school principals, but rather "leaders" who were imbued with the spirit of National Socialism.[48]

Schirach also sought to implement his program within the KLV.[49] To accomplish this, the "Reich Headquarters of the Reich Leader for the Expanded KLV" was created in Berlin and staffed "with trustworthy male and female leaders from the Hitler Youth as well as other specially qualified personnel." It was decided that the six-to-ten-year-olds would be placed with families in rural areas; the ten-to-fourteen-year-olds would go into "communal camps," that is, youth hostels, rural school hostels, hotels, guest houses, village schools, or vacation camps owned by commercial firms. At the end of 1940, some 300,000 children had been taken to the country from their homes in big cities; more than half were placed in 1,938 camp communities. Otto Würschinger wrote, "At the start of 1941 the number of evacuated children and young people had already risen to 382,616; they had been brought to their receiving districts by 1,631 special trains and 58 boat transports. All of them came from districts in western and northern Germany that were threatened by air raids; among them were 180,000 ten-to-fourteen-year-old boys and girls from Berlin and Hamburg. At the end of 1943, when the KLV had its greatest expansion, about 1 million young people were placed in KLV camps. There were about 5,000 camps in operation; the number of youngsters at the various camps varied greatly. The smallest camp had 18 young people; the largest, 1,200." If you count mothers with little children who were put up in family homes (KLV Headquarters was also in charge of these), then, by realistic estimates, the operation comprised about "3 million children and young people."[50]

Transportation of the students in the care of the KLV management was free of charge, as was room and board. According to Jutta Rüdiger, medical care was handled by "726 camp doctors, 125 army doctors, 390 nurse's aides, 278 nurses, and 94 medical students." Statistics for 1941 say that "a total of 5,000 beds and 500 caregivers" were available in more than 100 emergency hospitals for those KLV participants who became ill. In addition, between 1940 and 1945, in Bad Podiebrad about "1,000 young and older women" were trained in a "school for housekeepers" to take charge of housekeeping and kitchens in the camps.[51] In the same town there was a "KLV Reich School" for male camp squad leaders and two similar schools for female camp squad leaders. By the end of 1942, 6,393 boys and 3,767 girls had taken fourteen-day training courses there to prepare them for their future leadership tasks. In 1941 a "KLV Werkschule" was even set up in Prague in which male and female camp teachers as well as camp squad leaders could familiarize themselves with various forms of leisure activities that were "imbued with the spirit of National Socialism."[52]

Instead of entrusting the management of the numerous KLV camps completely to the male and female teachers deputized by the National Socialist Teachers League, Schirach assigned camp squad leaders chosen by the Hitler Youth leadership to assist them; often they were only a few years older than the children and young people entrusted to their care. Usually the teachers only had morning classes to teach, whereas the camp squad leaders who were responsible for the "self-guidance" of the young people had to take charge for the rest of the day and night.[53] They supervised morning rituals, cleanliness inspections, roll calls, physical training, singing and marching, field exercises, as well as political indoctrination.[54] In practice, teachers in KLV camps for younger children often assumed leadership roles in spite of unfavorable camp conditions. On the other hand, in camps with twelve-to-fifteen-year-olds, in which the camp squad leaders had already graduated from high school, teachers often had to be content with the subordinate roles assigned to them, particularly if they were retired secondary school teachers who had been posted to camp duty in lieu of a rest.[55] That doesn't mean that those camps in which the teachers had a greater say than the camp squad leaders were necessarily better or more humane. There were also vicious Nazis among the teachers who acted like tyrannical monsters. And there were sensible as well as malicious camp squad leaders, depending on whether they performed their assigned role or whether they despotically misused the position of power.

Because of the uncertainty as to who had what authority, it isn't easy to make generalizations with regard to the KLV camps between 1940 and 1945.[56] Whether the atmosphere that prevailed was caring or tyrannical depended on the circumstances in each camp. Almost every form of behavior existed in the camps: paternal or maternal solicitude, trust in the inherent goodness of human beings, naive idealism, as well as fascistic indoctrination, dreary routine, conscious brutalization, and the worst sort of sadism. Yet despite these countless variations, especially with regard to ideological, moral, and psychological factors, the emphasis here must be on the negative rather than the positive aspects of these camps—in contrast to the accounts of National Socialists such as Gerhard Dabel, Otto Würschinger, and Jutta Rüdiger, who in their descriptions of the KLV still grieved nostalgically for the political convictions of their youth. In the final analysis, the experiences in the camps were traumatic for many of those who stayed in them, as one can find out by talking with former KLV participants. There are probably several reasons why this darker aspect has been so neatly suppressed or glossed over up to now. These reasons should at last be brought out into the open.

It is easy to understand the teachers' silence about the role they played in these camps.[57] Later, after the war, like the great majority of Nazis, they didn't want to admit their participation, or they claimed that their main goal was to "prevent something worse [from happening]." The only former teachers who have spoken publicly about their work in the KLV are the naive, innocent ones, the "good people." For that reason their descriptions of the KLV are most frequently quoted by Dabel and Larass. In contrast, the "bad" teachers, that is, the fanatical Party members and those Party followers who were only out for their own advantage, have carefully covered their tracks. Moreover, the former camp squad leaders have not done any public work of mourning, but have remained silent too. Indeed, surviving members of these two groups won't discuss the KLV phenomenon, not even privately.

Thus, the only ones who might speak up are those who

participated as children and young people. But they too shy away from discussing their experiences frankly. Why? Are they still afraid of former camp squad leaders who might take umbrage at their descriptions of the camps? Probably. But it is not just these fears that have made honest discussion of the KLV experience taboo. Many people simply find their memories of those years "uncomfortable" and prefer to repress or dismiss them. But what sense is there in this kind of repression today? Wouldn't it be better to come to terms with the phenomenon and to draw up a detailed report of the experiences that would serve as a clear warning for the future? After all, although the years from 1940 to 1945 were years in which the "Expanded KLV" saved many children and young people from dying in air raids, as Mildred Scheel wrote later, they were also "a terrible, a truly terrible time" for those who were subjected to the political indoctrination and brutal training methods, something one "would not wish on any succeeding generation."[58]

But what is the best way to put together a report on all of this?[59] Since it's only in exceptional cases that children and young people leave behind usable written documents, one has to rely to a large extent on one's own recollections. And, as everyone knows, memory is often deceptive. However conscientiously one tries to remember those times, most people (and I include myself among them) interpret facts and events; they arrange the past into as meaningful or at least as coherent a sequence as possible so that a story develops, moving from the obscure to the clear, from the dark to the light, from something raw and unfinished into something mature and developed.[60] Thus such reconstructions seem to be ruled either by the principle *per aspera ad astra* or by the process of metamorphosis that Goethe presented paradigmatically in *Dichtung und Wahrheit*. Of course one may also depict one's childhood as a "sunny past" or even as a lost paradise—with one's subsequent life going steadily downhill, a descent into the misery of political, social, and psychological conflict. But ever since Freud exposed the problematic nature of childhood, this has become more rare. In any case, it would hardly be appropriate for people whose childhood was spent under German fascism. Indeed, people of this generation often fall into the opposite trap. They paint their youth in a purely negative light, characterizing themselves as sacrificial lambs in order to avoid a long overdue coming to terms with their past. I shall try to stay clear of such pitfalls as much as possible in this book.

Even so, what can a single and thus random reappraisal of the KLV experience accomplish? After all, this phenomenon affected the fate of millions of people. Still even an autobiographical account can rise above the merely personal—for if it adjusts to the framework of contemporary history, it can be at once a history of everyday life, of a society, of a nation, and of the mentality of a people. Moreover, my experience covers not just one, but five camps, each quite different from the others. I saw a broad cross-section of the various forms of the "Expanded KLV" between 1940 and 1945: First, a camp clearly stamped by the spirit of the Hitler Youth, like the one in Kirchenpopowo (today Popowo Koscielna) in what was then the Warthegau (October 1940–August 1941). Then, I stayed in a camp in San Remo, Italy' (June–August 1942), where concerned care predominated and which most resembled the picture of KLV camps painted by Dabel and Larass. The next camp was the KLV camp in Gross-Ottingen (Opoczki), also in the Warthegau (June 1943–September 1944), which was characterized almost exclusively by paramilitary training and sexual sadism. So when I was sent to an SS ski-training course on the Hohe Eule in Silesia (March-April 1944), it seemed to me almost like a pleasant vacation despite the premilitary drill. In contrast, at my last KLV camp in Sulmierschütz (Sulmirzyce) in the Warthegau (October 1944-January 1945), a mood of general hopelessness and anxiety already prevailed. Thus, not only did I have ordinary and even "beautiful" experiences in the KLV, but I was also exposed to its most brutal aspects. These ordeals may have been exceptional in their harshness, but just because of that they are especially instructive about the fascist educational programs in these camps.

This, then, comprises the historical and epistemological framework of my subject. But how does one flesh out the contents? I remember most vividly factual details of various camp situations. Some of these are relatively easy to talk about. But I shy away from describing those that involve sexual sadism. Nonetheless, rather than simply stringing the simple facts together, one must discuss this sexual element, because that is perhaps where the conscious trend to savagery in some of the camps manifested itself most clearly. It will probably be hardest to describe the fears, the feelings of shame and of desire, the psychological disorders, the inferiority complexes, and the suffering they brought on. How can I remember, for instance, what I "really" felt as a thirteen-to-fifteen-year-old in response to physical mistreatment, excessive tests of courage, adolescent sexual tortures, slaughter of animals, murder of Poles, and the sight of corpses? And even if I were to succeed in retrieving such feelings from the deep well of memory, how can impressions of this sort be rendered in words without taking them out of the realm of youthful experience and transposing them to a level of awareness beyond that of the child I was then?

One way of recapitulating these events is through a historically oriented description of personal experiences. Perhaps this would be the best way to present and analyze this vast but incomplete wealth of material, of remembered events. Therefore, in the following chapters, even when describing purely individual, indeed highly private experiences, I intend to deal also with their collective aspects. My descriptions of the various camps consequently should not be viewed only as a subjective portrayal, but also as paradigmatic of certain facets of the National Socialist educational system. Although throughout this book there are critical reflections that explode some myths and that deal with the difficulty of remembering, they are not a cover-up or designed to distract the reader from embarrassing details. On the contrary, they serve to take the account as a whole out of the particular and the arbitrary, broadening it to reflect the general. It is the explicit and implicit goal of this book to expose the political and social, as well as cultural, determinacy of the author-narrator; in the final analysis, this is a valid goal for all autobiographical writings concerned with a particular historical situation.[61] From this perspective, the first-person narrator is both the subjective creator of a report and also the objectifying historian who knows that he is the product of highly diverse social and psychological forces. Given his perplexity, he tries to present something that is more than merely a personal account.

Since this book deals almost exclusively with children and young people who had no part in the crimes committed by the Nazis and who were in some respects themselves victims of those crimes, the question of guilt or collective shame is not considered. My purpose is to offer as exact a description and examination as possible of the mechanisms of terror at work in the education of young people, of which Nazi fascism has provided the prime examples in recent German history. Therefore, to counter the abolition of history that is now pursued in the name of "modernization," this report about the KLV is dedicated to

Mnemosyne, the goddess of memory. It is intended to remind the reader of a simple truth expressed by Heinrich Böll: "A human being or a society without memory is sick."[62]

AFTER THE FIRST AIR RAIDS

KLV Camp Kirchenpopowo in the Warthegau
(Warthe District)

October 1940 – August 1941

▼

Memories can't be forced. They come to you spontaneous-
ly—or not at all. When childhood happenings elude recall,
you can never be sure whether the same psychological process that causes the forgetting of dreams is at work, or
whether these experiences have simply faded beyond recognition with the passage of time. For instance, I know
how very important the year 1940 was in my life, but this
knowledge doesn't help me much in clarifying the experiences of that time or tying them into a cohesive narrative.
Actually, they aren't much more than half-remembered,
half-interpreted mental images. This even applies to what I
thought were the three most decisive events of that year: at
Eastertime, at the age of ten, I entered secondary school;
shortly thereafter I became a *Pimpf* in the Jungvolk (a
member of the ten-to-fourteen-year-old group of the Hitler
Youth); and then in October I was shipped out of Berlin—
which was threatened by Allied air raids—to a KLV camp.[1]

I remember the change of schools best, since it obviously wasn't as traumatic an experience as the other events. I
had attended grammar school first in Johannisthal near
Niederschöneweide and then in Schmargendorf; in the
spring of 1940 the school administrator told my bewildered parents that I was now ready for secondary school.
My father was a poorly paid employee in a textile firm

who did not want to join the National Socialists, the Nazi Party. He had to provide for two children, his wife, and her mother, and so it seemed to him that my transfer to secondary school would be too expensive. But the Nazi school administrator talked it over with him, pointing to my good report cards, indeed even promising him financial assistance—and so he finally gave in.

Jost Hermand as a pupil in the first year (Sexta) at Paul von Hindenburg Secondary School (April 1940). From the author's collection.

Every morning starting in April 1940, I walked from our apartment at 4 Bingerstrasse to the Hindenburg Secondary School in Wilmersdorf. There I sat in a classroom with boys from both blue- and white-collar families. It was the workers' sons—who were being nurtured by the Nazis for their social Darwinist purposes—who set the tone, not the pampered sons of the bourgeoisie, as had been the case in the class society of the Weimar Republic. I was intimidated by the somewhat "coarse" atmosphere in the school. But in elementary school, especially in Niederschöneweide, the pupils' manners had been even rougher. So pretty soon I felt quite at home as a first-year (*Sexta*) student. A few school photos, in which I smile at the camera, seem to support this. Besides, the boys didn't tease me as mercilessly about my stutter as had the brats in elementary school. Moreover, the teachers were more understanding; they didn't thrash us when they happened to be overworked or in a bad mood.

As a shy ten-year-old with a speech impediment, I tried to make friends—as I had in elementary school—with the somewhat more "refined" boys in my class, preferring to avoid the raucous workers' children who were always pushing and shoving. I was encouraged in this by my mother, who had been brought up as a young lady but who had married "beneath her." Like her own impoverished mother who had once been a lady at the court in Weimar, she tried with all her might to hold on to former niceties and standards of behavior. My father, who came from the poorest of families, had little sympathy for all this. He sold fabrics during the day, and in the evenings, to augment his meager wages, he played the piano at various bars.

And so, from the outset I was caught in the middle, both at school and at home. Since I came from Niederschöneweide, I spoke the same dialect as the working-class children from eastern Berlin. But my mother, who was glad that I was now a high school student, pushed me relentlessly toward bourgeois things and wanted me to speak High German. She thought the Nazis too vulgar for words and strongly advised my father not to join the National Socialists. In fact, she even threatened to divorce him if he should sign up. She knew very well that joining the Party would have offered my father a chance for social advancement. But she had too much of what she called "inner dignity" to attain the respectability she so fervently yearned for through the back door. So she chose to stay poor and tried to face her lot with as much equanimity as possible. When I entered the new school, my mother—who had a way with people—met two teachers there who felt as she did and who reinforced her instinctive antipathy to the National Socialists. To some extent this eased her mind.

My mother had strong objections to the Hitler Youth. My brother, Fritz, who was three years older and considerably more vigorous than I, was raised by my paternal grandmother since my parents didn't have enough money to care for two children in the first ten years of their marriage. He resigned himself to joining the Hitler Youth relatively early; that is, he did what was expected of him and didn't let anything upset him. In general, my mother allowed him to do whatever he wanted. On the other hand, when I was inducted into the Jungvolk on 20 April, Hitler's birthday, and immediately began to pester her with complaints about the roughness of the other Pimpfs, she showed a great deal of understanding for my problems and indeed tried in every possible way to set me against the organization. However, since membership in the Hitler Youth was already mandatory at that time, she couldn't do much about the fact that I had to "report for duty" every Saturday afternoon and sometimes even on Wednesday afternoons. But at least she could make sure that I looked "smart" in my uniform. This got to be quite expensive since we also had to buy the accompanying knapsack, knife and scabbard, shoulder strap and leather belt, as well as the various insignia. My mother tried to keep me from picking up the Pimpfs' jargon while waiting for the day when she could find a reason to protest the brutality prevailing in the Jungvolk—both the excessive fighting and the severity of the pseudomilitary exercises. But it never came to that. Moreover, she knew that had she complained, she might very well have been arrested. And so she and I remained merely silent conspirators.

In the summer of 1940, I served in the "Stosstrupp" squad after I had memorized the Nazi dogma:[2]

Boys of the Jungvolk are tough,
Discreet, and true:
Boys of the Jungvolk are comrades.
The Jungvolk boy's highest ideal is his honor.

I also pledged allegiance to the flag: "He who swears an oath to the Führer's flag gives up everything he possesses." The *Jungzüge* (boys platoons) and *Jungenschaften* (boys squads) attached to this troop usually met at the Schmargendorfer Roseneck or at the Hundekehle in the Berlin Grunewald. In both those areas, there were still many places that had not been built up, overgrown stretches of woods where we carried out so-called field exercises. We had either red or blue woolen threads tied around our left upper arms. Each squad was ordered to find another squad within a predetermined area in a manner appropriate to cross-country maneuvers, that is, through military reconnaissance. Once the "enemy" squad was located, we were to rip the woolen threads off the other Pimpfs' arms, usually after drawn-out fist fights. This exercise was supposed to teach us that "comradeship," as they called it, is forged in battle. We also had to march a lot in the Stosstrupp troop while singing the prescribed Hitler Youth songs. But there was hardly any theoretical indoctrination at this level of the Jungvolk—in any case, I can't remember any. We did get together for *Heimabende*, evenings of instruction. What was specifically fascist in these Hitler Youth activities, which also included camping trips, was the attempt to toughen us up. The Nazis wanted to change us from limp "dishrags" into "real guys," to quote the *National Socialist Letters of Indoctrination* (*Schulungsbriefe*), which I actually read decades later. As late as 1983 Jutta Rüdiger wrote, "the Pimpfs were supposed to show that they weren't soft 'little mama's boys' who had everything done for them, but that they could tackle things on their own."[3] We participated in rituals such as hoisting the flag, marching drills, and roll calls, calculated to serve the same goals, and intended to wean us from all unboyish, "weak" activities and to engender in us a sense of the grand task that awaited us.

Leaving the big city. Propaganda photograph of the National Socialist Organization Kinderlandverschickung, 1937. From Neues Volk: Blätter des rassenpolitischen Amtes der NSDAP *(1937).*

My classmates and I were evacuated for the first time on 6 October 1940.[4] Obviously, it was all done in a great rush. Unfortunately, I no longer remember the process of packing my suitcase and what my reactions were. I think the only thing I recall clearly is the departure from a railway depot in eastern Berlin, probably the Lichtenberg station. I see myself as though I were a figure in one of those August 1914 farewell photos that appeared in many of the patriotic depictions of the First World War. I'm leaning out of the train compartment window with other boys; with my right hand I wave to my mother, who is standing below on the railway platform, fighting to keep back the tears. But this image is probably much too stereotypical to be true. Perhaps it only proves how conditioned we are to make our own, highly personal experiences fit the clichés of the collective experience. However, it is possible that everything happened just that way. In any case, today, as I write this, I clearly see in my mind's eye two people who have become strangers to me in the meantime: the bewildered ten-year-old and his seemingly calm and collected mother, trying not to show her heartache and smiling bravely so that her child won't know she is grieving as he starts out on his journey.

Our KLV train arrived the same day in Posen (Poznań), the capital of the Reich district (*Reichsgau*) Wartheland.[5] The next morning we continued on the same train toward Rogasen (Rogozno). There, the different school classes were separated and transported in buses to the camps that had been prepared for them. My brother and his class were taken to Lechlin; my class was sent to Kirchenpopowo, which some of my classmates immediately baptized "the asshole of the world"—a pun on the name Kirchenpopowo, which contains the German word *Popo*, a colloquial term for backside—because of its remoteness and ugliness. Kirchenpopowo, which had been officially renamed "Geroldsfeld" by the Nazis, consisted of some twenty houses and was located in a largely German-speaking part of the Warthegau, so we could easily walk from the old schoolhouse where we were quartered to the village without running into any hostile Poles.[6] Life in this village was quite relaxed, at first glance almost peaceful. In contrast to Berlin, there were as yet no food coupons or other rationing, no shortage of meat and eggs. So some of us, with the money we had brought along, immediately bought things that were scarce at home and mailed them to our parents. I clearly remember, for instance, filling two pairs of socks with several pounds of sugar, wrapping them up well, and sending them off to my mother. There was also plenty of fruit, especially apples, pears, and late raspberries.

Our gym teacher, Mr. Zinsel, had been appointed director of the camp. He was assisted, in a subordinate position, by Dr. Erwin Fette, our biology teacher, whom I especially liked because of his love for animals. I have no good memories of Mr. Zinsel. He was probably an ardent Nazi, but no doubt saw us first-year secondary school pupils as mere boys who did not yet have the necessary understanding for the noble tasks of the new Reich. Consequently, he didn't torture us with racial theories or other specifically fascist themes. Instead he taught us German grammar and the fundamentals of simple fractions. But as the months went by, he lost interest in teaching and devoted himself to his administrative functions and his family, who were also living in the camp.

In contrast, Dr. Fette had plenty of time for us. He was in his forties, a bachelor, and a superb teacher. Opposed to the Nazi ideology, he taught us almost all the subjects his colleague didn't want to teach. He was especially fond of plants and animals, and he tried to instill in us a respect for them. Since he quickly discovered my interest in biology, he encouraged me whenever I came across any wildflowers or birds to enter their names systematically, that is, alphabetically, in a black notebook. In the spring of 1941, Dr. Fette was indignant when the camp director sent us into the surrounding marsh meadows to collect lapwing eggs, which the director considered a special delicacy. On such occasions Dr. Fette's face would turn beet-red, a condition he attributed to having been thrown into the air by an explosion that occurred on the ship on which he was serving as a young naval officer toward the end of World War I. Ever since, he said, he had suffered from seizures brought on by stressful situations. In addition to biology, he was also very interested in geography. To arouse our own interest in the subject, Dr. Fette sent us, two or three at a time, to the village to measure all the houses and plots of land. Under his direction, we used these measurements to make a scale map of Kirchenpopowo. When it was finished, we felt extraordinarily proud of our first scientific accomplishment.

In the few photos I have of my time in this camp, I am nearly always wearing the Jungvolk winter uniform, indicating that we did regular Hitler Youth duty on afternoons and weekends. The camp squad leader in charge was named either Flotow or Kleinau. I no longer remember whether he was particularly rigid or exploited his power in a tyrannical way. Since he was only three or four years older than we were (which counts a lot at this age), he would hardly have been in a position to introduce us to

The Führer's birthday in KLV Camp Kirchenpopowo, 20 April 1941. Photograph by Jürgen Welzel.

Nazi racial theories. He probably required us, as was usual for the Hitler Youth service, to sing songs and march back and forth for hours on end, just as the leader of the boys' platoon in the Stosstrupp troop had done. In addition, he was responsible for a weeklong camping trip and for organizing the ceremony to celebrate Hitler's birthday. But I have only vague memories of these events.

In contrast, I remember the incessant physical training exercises in great detail. Because I wasn't particularly athletic, they were very hard on me. Luckily our camp didn't have sports equipment like horizontal or parallel bars; I had failed miserably to master these in the Hindenburg high school gym, where the other boys used to make fun of me, calling me "spider monkey" because of my awkwardness. But in Kirchenpopowo we did have *Völkerball*, which I'd already come to hate in Berlin. This is a game played by two opposing teams, in which the players try to take their opponents out by hitting them with the ball. Before a game started, lots would be drawn to select two team captains who, taking turns, chose their players from the pool of boys. I was frequently the last one to be picked since nobody really wanted me on their team; but eventually— accompanied by laughter all around—I was assigned to one side or the other.

Most of the boys had a great time in sports. Many spent the entire morning waiting impatiently for the moment in the afternoon when they could run out to the courtyard behind the school and begin playing Völkerball. During the game the weaker boys were chased like rabbits across the field by the ace players with their mighty throwing arms. Over time this wild roughhousing—along with the eternal marching—contributed to a marked brutalizing of many of the boys. Even Dr. Fette couldn't effectively counteract it, although he tried by assigning more homework, recommending good books for us to read, and taking us on nature hikes.

Most of the boys had respect only for those of their peers who boasted a lot, could show budding biceps, could get their way by brute force, and who mercilessly tyrannized the weaker boys, in short, for boys who were "quick as a greyhound, tough as leather, and hard as Krupp steel." And so, despite all the myths about the camaraderie of the Hitler Youth, no such spirit prevailed in the three dormitories that also served as our living rooms. Instead, there was a firmly established pecking order in which each boy was very much aware of his assigned position. Everybody knew exactly whose shoes he had to shine and who in turn would shine his, whose homework he had to do and who would do his for him, even which of the boys he had to satisfy manually at night and who had to satisfy him. I don't know how much Mr. Zinsel and the camp squad leader knew of this ranking system. But even had they been aware of it, as fascist educators committed to the principles of "toughening-up and the selection of the fittest," they would certainly not have taken any steps to discourage it.

We all aspired to move up in this pecking order, so as not to be held in contempt by most of the other boys. I know that this is not only a fascist aspiration, and that it plays a key role in many boarding schools. Novels like Robert Musil's *Die Verwirrungen des Zöglings Törless* (*Young Törless*) (1906) and Ernst von Salomon's *Die Kadetten* (The cadets) (1933), as well as the English film *If* (1969) by Lindsay Anderson, describe this atmosphere in the revered "public" schools. But over and above the perceived rigor of the training and the sexual sadism prevalent in many boarding schools, there was one aspect of the KLV camp in Kirchenpopowo that is comprehensible only when seen against the backdrop of the educational principles of National Socialism, namely, the total lack of any utopian ideas. Whereas earlier boarding schools, even with all their severity and discipline, had always advocated certain values—Christian, nationalistic, humanistic, or those of some organization—in Kirchenpopowo no ideals of any sort were imparted to us except the necessity of toughness and self-assertion. We children were left mostly to our own devices, as Hitler and Schirach had demanded. The National Socialists knew full well that in a social Darwinist contest of strength it would not be Rousseau's Noble Savages who would triumph but rather the hard individuals, the physically superior, the future "leaders."

For a boy like me who was a good student but had no skill in sports, this meant being at the bottom third of the hierarchy that evolved within the camp. In the interest of self-preservation I did my best to keep from sinking even lower; that is, I tried as hard as I could to qualify for a better spot in the social hierarchy. But there were many barriers to overcome. One of them was my stutter, which was considered a sign of weakness, of softness, if not outright failure. That is why I was both overjoyed and at the same time utterly dismayed when my mother suddenly turned up in Kirchenpopowo in the spring of 1941. She was the first mother who had ventured to visit the camp and thought herself quite daring.[7] But this invasion of our KLV world was very embarrassing for me because it was immediately interpreted by the other boys as a sign of my dependency and weakness. As a result, I fell back at least two rungs on the ladder. Of course, it never occurred to me that there might have been another reason for my mother's visit to Kirchenpopowo. She had also come to see Dr. Fette, whom she had met in Berlin in the summer of 1940 and who also had antifascist leanings. For a few days my mother stayed in the back room of the Geroldsfeld postmistress's house, where she was almost raped one night by a German soldier. After a few days, I managed to persuade her to leave so that the other boys would stop making fun of me. With permission from the camp director, she took me along on a two-day trip, first to Posen and then to visit my brother in Lechlin. After that we spent another day in Schocken (Skoki), where we surreptitiously went swimming in the lake after dark. Then we parted, but not before I gave her a detailed description of conditions in the camp, imploring her not to tell anyone.

Luckily, my mother's visit didn't do me as much damage as I had feared. After she broke the ice, other mothers also came to Kirchenpopowo, so that pretty soon I was no longer the only "mama's boy." Still, I wasn't able to improve my standing within the camp (or at any rate among the boys in my room). Until the end of my stay, I continued to be at the low end of the pecking order. Although I was not despised as much as Michaelis, a shy and constantly embarrassed boy who occupied the bunk next to mine, I was not held in the same esteem as the athletic kings of the Völkerball games who had the bunk beds above ours. I had no real friend in that camp, although I would have liked that. A friendship would have protected me from disrespect as well as overt molestation. But my speech defect made it impossible for me to express my feelings or even to initiate a conversation that might lead to friendship. Sometimes, when I tried, I was barely able to finish what I was saying. I was considered a loser from whom you couldn't expect much as either friend or protector.

Also, the good relationship I had with Dr. Fette kept me from having a better rapport with the other boys. He was the only trustworthy person in that camp—and some of the other boys would have thought themselves lucky to be on such good terms with him. He showed his preference for me only when I was alone with him in the afternoons, and he would tell me about the "wonders" of the animal and plant world. In public he treated me as he did all the other boys. Yet in a situation in which no one trusts anyone, not even the most circumspect behavior is much help. And so I finally came to be considered Dr. Fette's "pet" and was envied by the other boys. Once Dr. Fette found out about this, he no longer paid as much attention to me, and I lost him as a fatherly friend without winning the friendship of any of my classmates.

Conversations among us boys rarely went beyond childish grumbling, bad-mouthing others, furious personal attacks, and arrogant bragging. With the exception of Dr. Fette and his efforts to have us share his love of nature, no one imbued us with any concrete ideals, that is, no one encouraged camaraderie or extolled National Socialism. Our behavior was mostly marked by an infantile and aggressive egoism directed toward self-assertion and pleasure. The most important topic of conversation for us boys in Kirchenpopowo was sex, especially after dark. Once we were in our beds, those who had read illustrated sex education manuals would describe new positions and situations, arousing everyone in the room to such a degree that soon one could hear the rhythmic sounds of masturbation. None of us had yet reached the age of puberty, so it was possible to come to a so-called climax without ejaculation, which would have drained you and made you sleepy. Consequently, these exercises could be repeated over and over, often lasting far into the night.

In time things got out of hand and contributed to a noticeable dullness and general apathy. We paid less and less attention to the lessons being dished out to us during school hours, and even the slogans of our camp director and the Hitler Youth squad leader scarcely interested us anymore. We were increasingly preoccupied with our bodies: Völkerball, field exercises, washing, and the constant manipulation of our genitalia. Without any mental or cultural stimulation, without the mediation of a social identity, without instruction in the biological function of our pleasurable physical sensations, we were allowed to regress into a primitive physicality. But before things reached the point of sadistic excesses, before reciprocal masturbation took on violent aspects, KLV Camp Geroldsfeld, as it was now called, was suddenly closed in August 1941. In the preceding months, the powerful air defense provided by Reich Air Force Commander-in-Chief Hermann Göring had forced the British to break off their nighttime bombing raids on Berlin. The reason for the evacuation of all schoolchildren from the city, ordered by Hitler at the end of September 1940, no longer existed.

But when we arrived at Lichtenberg Station on 10 August, we were not the same boys who—confused and curious—had left for the unknown East nine months earlier. Some of the boys, especially those from "good" upper-middle-class families, were belatedly ashamed of the lasciviousness unleashed in the camp, and they resolved from now on to live more ascetic lives. Even the tougher boys had some guilt feelings, which—out of fear of their parents—they tried to hide as best they could. I certainly was remorseful. But I confided in my mother, and she understood my needs; as a result, our relationship improved. Indeed, she made every effort to make my reintegration into everyday school and family life as easy as possible. To her dismay, however, I came down with scarlet fever two weeks after my return. Confined to bed for almost a month, I hovered between life and death. Once I felt better, my mother took me to Sellin on the island of Rügen in the Baltic Sea for a short period of recuperation. She had heard there were boardinghouses on the island with cheap off-season rates. But after we had been there only a week, a local doctor found that the scarlet fever had resulted not only in a cardiac valve defect but also in serious rheumatic fever. Concerned for my health in Sellin's cold and unremittingly rainy weather, my mother took me back to Berlin.

Although I can remember my time in Kirchenpopowo

with its many demeaning and arduous experiences only in scattered fragments, I've scarcely forgotten anything about the months I spent in my mother's loving care. It was like waking up from a bad dream you want to push out of your mind as quickly as possible. And while I was sick, I put myself completely in her hands and resolved that from then on I would live up to her idea of a good son and an industrious student. Every morning I scrubbed myself thoroughly, twice a day I brushed my teeth, I polished my shoes, promptly removed stains from my trousers or jacket with a washcloth dipped in cold water, and did my homework in the early afternoon rather than waiting till late in the evening. For a while all this was even fun because it wasn't done out of fear of the camp squad leader, but rather out of gratitude to my mother.

In the months that followed, what bothered me most was my membership in what my mother and I called the "horrible" Hitler Youth. I was making rapid progress in school and, even though I was only in the second year (*Quinta*) of high school, Dr. Fette had appointed me biology monitor; it was my job during recess to feed the fish, the axolotl, and the spotted salamanders. However, I found service in the Jungvolk a meaningless torture that reminded me of my worst KLV camp experiences. I was assigned to the "Death Wolves" (*Totenwölfe*) squad, and just as in the "Stosstrupp" squad and at camp, we had to memorize snappy repetitive verses and sing pathos-laden marching songs. The following two verses, which sharply attack the dapper sons of the middle class, appeared at the top of one of the best-known Jungvolk manifestos and are indicative of the mood the words and songs were supposed to inspire in us:

Heated rooms
and cigarettes,
golden rings,
starched cuffs,

perfumed soaps
and sweet boys
with pallid faces;
we don't want *them!*

We are Pimpfs
with wild manes
and hard fists,
with hobnailed boots
and laughing teeth;
we accomplish things
and do not rest.
Whether rich or poor,
we are all equal.[8]

What I found even more dreadful than these songs were the brutal field exercises. Something that two years before had been childish jostling now almost always degenerated into general free-for-alls that resulted not only in bumps and bruises but in scrapes and more severe injuries. In addition to "instructing [us] in the use of maps and compasses, delivering messages, estimating distances, target identification, and terrain evaluation" as is spelled out in Günter Kaufmann's *Das kommende Deutschland* (The future Germany), games like these were above all supposed to turn us into ruthless "warriors."[9] Therefore we were repeatedly urged by our platoon leaders not to show any pity for our "opponents" and to bring down anyone who opposed us with a hook to the jaw, or to hold him in a headlock until he ran out of steam or gave up. For those boys who were strong, this was carte blanche to mercilessly beat up the smaller and weaker ones among us, and to derive sadistic pleasure from such acts. Most of the time, my only recourse was to hide behind a tree or dense shrubbery and wait for the whistle that signaled the end of the game. I escaped some beatings that way, but then when I was caught, the beatings were that much worse.

The merciless nature of these field exercises is corrobo-

Jost and Fritz Hermand in Hitler Youth uniforms on a street in Berlin (spring 1942). From the author's collection.

rated by several Jungvolk books from those years, which read almost like "battlefield diaries."[10] One, a novel by Alfred Weidemann called *Jungzug 2: Fünfzig Jungen im Dienst* (Boys' Platoon No. 2: Fifty boys serving their country), was presented as a factual account; in 1937 it was declared the "best Jungvolk book" by Deputy Reich Youth Leader Hermann Lauterbacher. Even today I can recall entire passages from it; I probably heard it read aloud at one of my platoon's instructional evenings. The book describes with stirring realism the encounter between two young platoons in the course of a field exercise planned by their leaders: "Hardi had just returned from a raid, and he quickly gathered his boys for an attack. And now as the enemy got closer and closer, he gave the signal to attack. The tremendous force of the encounter pushed the Browns back. The fighters rushed at one another in a confused tangle and crowded around the metal buckets which were what the fight was all about [the buckets were the trophies they had to win]. The fellows pull each other down onto the ground in fighting clumps. Hardi is everywhere. He leaves bumps and bruises wherever he lands a blow. Wolf is fighting his way toward him and soon they're going at each other. You can't tell anymore to whom the legs and feet belong that are now so wildly flailing and kicking. Fists drum furiously on hard young heads—the buttons start to pop off their pants—afraid, they try to protect their bellies from wild hobnailed boots. Three drawn-out whistle blasts are heard above the panting, yelling, and screaming. Sissi is signaling the end of the war game. No way! Their shirts are already torn! The beating and kicking continues furiously. Wolf tears himself from the tangle and calls his men back. The boys' hair is in wild disarray and their faces are flushed from the fighting."[11]

When I told my mother how terrible my service with the Totenwölfe was, and above all, how scared I was during the field exercises, she moved heaven and earth to get me out of that troop. Although it wasn't easy, it didn't take her very long to do it. After that, in the spring of 1942, I was transferred to the Steglitz music squad. The leader there pressed a valveless trumpet into my hand. Just like that I was expected to join the other much more advanced Pimpfs in playing the "Hohenfriedberger March" or something like it.[12] But in June 1942, before I could blow my first note on that trumpet, I was evacuated again and sent to my second camp.

THE FÜHRER'S ACT OF GENEROSITY
The KLV Camp in San Remo, Italy

June–August 1942

▼

It was a stroke of luck that landed me in my second camp. In May 1942 all the high schools for boys in Berlin were asked to pick a talented but poor third/fourth-year (*Tertianer*) student in need of a vacation at a health resort. For this, Hitler was making his own villa in San Remo, Italy, available for three months. I fulfilled all the requirements. According to a journal I kept at the time, my mother was notified to deliver me to the San Remo Special Detail (*Sonderkommando*) at the Potsdam train station on 1 June at 8:30 A.M. I was to bring my Hitler Youth uniform and some regular clothes. The Special Detail consisted of a woman camp commander, a Hitler Youth leader, and a nurse. Altogether twenty-five boys, strangers to one another, were being sent to this camp. After a long train ride—my first—we spent the next night in a small hotel in Munich. The following morning the train crossed the Brenner Pass, went through Verona, then Milan and Genoa. We finally arrived in San Remo late in the evening of the second day, totally exhausted from the long trip and the nearly tropical Italian heat. The housekeeper of the Villa Zirio picked us up at the train station.

The villa turned out to be extremely luxurious and spacious. To us, coming mostly from four- or five-story tenements, the house and its parklike grounds with white stone benches and pergolas seemed "swell" (*dufte*), and that became our most-used adjective in the weeks that followed. Two or three boys were assigned to a room. On waking up the next day, we ran over to the windows to marvel at all the different kinds of palm trees, agaves, and other exotic plants growing on the grounds, things we had so far only learned about in biology class. It was just as hot as the day before, and in the three months we spent there it never got much cooler. We were quite unprepared for this heat.

In the 1880s, we were told, the villa had belonged to the German crown prince who later became Emperor Frederick III. He had tuberculosis of the larynx, and after the death of his father he held his exalted position only a few months before he also died.[1] Later the villa became the property of Benito Mussolini, who in the thirties signed it over to his friend Adolf Hitler. And now we were living there—twenty-five Berlin urchins, who had never before slept in rooms with genuine stucco ornamentation, hot- and cold-running water, and in beds with silk coverlets. That first night we felt we were in never-never land.

But it wasn't just the rooms of the villa that were "swell"; all our days were ideal. After a long, restful sleep, we were served a "hotel breakfast" at eight o'clock, with honey, jam, sausage, and a boiled egg. Instead of having to bone up on math or Latin, we ran down to the beach. However, we were allowed to swim for only fifteen minutes because the camp director assured us the water was much too salty and staying in it longer would be too exhausting for us. Then we were served an opulent noonday meal, after which we either rested, went into the garden, or played various board games: *Mühle* (Morris), *Dame* (checkers), *Halma* (Chinese checkers), and a few times even *Mensch ärg're dich nicht*, though that was considered a childish game. For a while this sort of life was pretty appealing, but then it began to get boring. At that point our Hitler Youth squad leader intervened. I must say, I have as little recollection of him as of the camp squad leader in Kirchenpopowo. The first few days we had been wearing everyday clothes, but on weekends we had to put on our summer uniforms and practice singing and marching. As experienced Pimpfs and KLV participants, we raised no objections.

Our first marches took us into the environs of San Remo. There were organized singing contests with *Gioventù*, the local fascist youth organization whose members also showed up in their uniforms. Although the Italian boys sang with a good deal more gusto than we did, our Hitler Youth camp squad leader encouraged us to think that we were better than "those Italianos." Moreover, after we had marched through the picturesque but somewhat dilapidated and noisy old town, whose streets stank from the contents of emptied chamber pots, he pointed out to us that in Germany, thanks to Hitler, such conditions did not exist anymore. And we believed him, even though many of us came from very modest circumstances indeed. Our squad leader had probably grown up in a posh Berlin suburb like Schlachtensee. Of course, poverty was considerably less visible in Berlin than in Italy, where life—because of the warmer climate—took place mostly on the streets.

Otherwise our Nazi indoctrination was limited or carried out in such a way that we did not even perceive it as such. All week long we looked forward to marching to the movie house on Sunday morning to watch the films that had been picked by the Nazi propaganda office for young people of our age. I have forgotten many of them. Only a few films like *Der grosse König* (The great king), *Hitlerjunge Quex* (Hitler Youth Quex), *Die Entlassung* (When [Bismarck] was fired), . . . *reitet für Deutschland* ([He] rides for Germany), and *Quax, der Bruchpilot* (Quax, hard-luck pilot) still echo in my memory. We watched these films attentively, but they did not promote feelings of solidarity as some people later claimed.[2] My recollection of the weekly newsreels that preceded the feature is somewhat clearer. Most of them were "old"; that is, we were shown clips of the 1941–42 winter campaign against the Soviet Union. I no longer remember how we reacted, politically or emotionally, to the events presented in these films. But I do remember how agreeable it was to see all that snow on the screen while sitting in that stifling movie house. After all, in those days there was scarcely anything one could do to get relief from the heat: there were no air conditioners, refrigerators, iced drinks, or delicious ice cream sundaes. After a series of such newsreels, in which it was always the German troops who performed the "heroic deeds," we felt less and less respect for the Italians. Even the Italian soldiers we sometimes saw on the rocks by the sea, singing heart-rending melancholy songs, were contemptuously described by the camp squad leader and the camp director as "soft." What they lacked, we were told, was "snappiness." This, in a camp where we were supposed to be recuperating, not briskly or snappily, but as tranquilly as possible.

At the end of July I learned what real "heroes" looked like when I developed an ear infection and was taken to a nearby villa that had been turned into a German hospital. The Villa Maddalena was situated somewhat farther up the hill than our villa, as I found out recently by checking in an old Baedeker. During the two weeks I spent there under doctor's care, I shared a room with an officer who was a member of the parachutists and a recipient of the German Knight's Cross. He had lost his left leg during a parachute jump over Crete in the summer of 1941. For months the doctors had been trying various treatments on him because the stump refused to heal. This young first lieutenant was exceptionally charming. He would talk with me for hours on end and didn't seem to mind my stutter. And so after only a few days, I came to admire him and to envy his fate as well as the solicitous care that was lavished on him by everyone. From the time I started school I had dreamt how nice it must be to be pitied by everyone for having lost a leg or being blind, instead of having people secretly smirk at my stuttering. There was only one thing I didn't approve of—the lieutenant was constantly flirting with his Italian nurse and enjoyed having her sit on his bed. It seemed to me that such behavior wasn't appropriate for a German officer, especially one I liked so much. I was inconsolable when ten days later, with my ear infection cured, I had to say good-bye to my idol and go back to the camp.

Nothing much had changed at Villa Zirio while I was gone. It was still hot, the daily routine as dreary as before, and the swimming time allotted to us still too short. To lift our spirits, the camp director finally proposed that we have a social evening, including a variety show, to celebrate the end of our stay in the camp. We weren't very enthusiastic about the idea. Still, the rehearsals for the individual numbers were considerably more diverting than the constant marching and the rigidly enforced periods of bed rest. The variety show took place in the entrance hall of the villa. Naturally we sang the usual Hitler Youth songs, but there were also a series of short skits and charades, some of which I still remember for their idiotic innocence.

At the end of August we took the train back to Berlin— and I never again saw any of the boys who had been with me in San Remo, where people lived almost as if there were no war, where there were no air raids and no food rationing cards. In contrast, the mood in Berlin was very depressed. Through the spring of 1942, reports of victories had followed one after the other on the radio; now the news was more and more often about offensives that had bogged down, about "tactical realignments," and about the first German defeats. The report at the end of November 1942 that the German Afrika Korps had retreated after the Battle of El Alamein presaged the war's course. A short time later Soviet troops penetrated the Romanian front and encircled the German Sixth Army at Stalingrad. Simultaneously, German occupation forces in Greece and Yugoslavia were facing increasingly resourceful maneuvers by the resistance groups. Then in January 1943, the German and Italian troops in Tripoli were forced to surrender, and the remainder of the Sixth Army was captured by the Soviets at Stalingrad. In the face of these defeats and to combat increasing indignation among the civilian population, Goebbels issued a declaration of "total war" on 17 February 1943.

While all this was going on, I had to go to school in Wilmersdorf and attend the mandatory Hitler Youth meetings as though nothing had happened. I clearly remember the instruction in school. Because more and more of the male teachers were being sent to the front, we were now also taught by women. One of them, who was a fanatical Nazi, or perhaps she was only doing her assigned duty, taught our German class and also introduced us to racial studies. Under her direction we read the novel, *König Geiserich* (1936), by the Nazi writer Hans Friedrich Blunck, which described the heroic decline of the Vandals in North Africa.[3] I read the Blunck book avidly, as I was beginning to feel that Karl May novels were too "mindless." By that time I had become more interested in historical books, having already devoured Werner Beumelburg's novel *Kaiser und Herzog* (Emperor and duke) (1936). On the whole, most of us had no objections to the racial studies classes. They only became an embarrassment for me when, in the course of her explanation of the Nordic racial type, the teacher asked me to stand up and pointed to my "ash blond" hair, my "deep blue" eyes, and the "length" of the back of my skull. The other pupils began to giggle. When entering the school, I had had to hand in a detailed genealogical chart because of my French name (d'Hermand). So it came as a surprise to find out that I was a real "German" type.

Something similar happened to me in the Steglitz band,

where I was again enrolled among the trumpeters after my return from San Remo. Because I was blond, I always had to stand in the front row, whereas the dark-haired boys were posted to the rear. Playing my trumpet, no matter how beautifully it gleamed, was a nightmare from the start. I couldn't produce a single tone from this valveless metal contraption since we never had individual lessons but were simply lined up in rank and file and told to blow. And so I only pretended to play: I puffed out my cheeks but allowed no air to enter the mouthpiece, hoping that no one would notice. Luckily, no one ever did, probably because there were more than forty trumpeters. After a few weeks, some of the boys who were quite a bit stronger and more self-confident could blow pretty well. And so the initial earsplitting cacophony gradually turned into sequential notes that sounded something like the "Hohenfriedberger March."

Once the trumpeters got good enough and the drummers could bang their giant drums properly, things turned serious. From October 1942 on, we no longer did our monotonous trumpeting in any old deserted space; instead we were often called on by the top Party leadership to play for "festive occasions." I remember one of these times especially clearly. Mussolini was expected in Berlin on a state visit, and our band was supposed to assemble in front of the Anhalter train station. After we'd been standing there, waiting, for three hours (I, as usual, in the front row), Hitler and Il Duce finally came out of the station and Hitler asked us to play a march. As always, I was pretending to play—this time only ten steps away from Hitler—and sweating bullets. Instead of being proud to be participating in such a gala ceremony, I was panic-stricken that the Führer might ask me to step forward and play a solo. Fortunately, that didn't happen. We merely held our trumpets at our sides and had our hands shaken by both leaders to the accompaniment of clicking camera shutters. For days afterward I was convinced everyone was on to me and calmed down only when I heard there was another boy in the band who also only pretended to play—although I never got up the nerve to talk to him about it.

In addition to playing in the Steglitz band, in the winter of 1942–43 I was enlisted by the Hitler Youth to collect money in an intensified drive for contributions to the Winter Relief (*Winterhilfswerk*) and the National Socialist People's Welfare (*Nationalsozialistische Volkswohlfahrt*). We Pimpfs were given large bags of enameled pins—usually colorful butterflies—which we were supposed to offer to prospective contributors either on the street or going from door to door. That winter the Nazis were already being

Hitler and a Hitler Youth trumpeter in Nurenberg (1933). From H. W. Koch, Hitler Youth: The Duped Generation (New York: Ballantine Books, 1972).

THE FÜHRER'S ACT OF GENEROSITY

criticized quite openly by some people, and some of the passersby expressed indignation at these constant solicitations. After the autumn of 1942, my mother also ripped into the Nazi "boss rule." My father, who didn't think much of the National Socialist system either, but who had to be a lot more careful because he might lose his job, warned her often to control herself and not to endanger him and the whole family by her combative attitude. Nevertheless, my mother wasn't intimidated by his reproaches, and this caused repeated political and also personal arguments between my parents.

I remember one of these confrontations in particular. My parents had invited Dr. Fette and a man named Schröder, a Nazi from the Ministry of Agriculture, to dinner at our house. To save money for the evening, we had been eating "one-pot" meals (usually a cheap stew) all week. Dr. Fette started the quarrel by recounting indignantly that an eighteen-year-old girl had recently told him she had been asked by the League of German Girls not to be too prudish toward soldiers on leave from the front. In the first place, she was told, these men had been risking their lives for the fatherland for years and needed to experience "something nice for a change" during their short leaves; and second, as the Führer had said, the Germany of the future would need many more children than ever before. Mr. Schröder, who was imbued with high moral values but was also a deeply convinced Party member, was so enraged by Dr. Fette's comments that he threatened both him and my mother—who had sprung to Dr. Fette's defense— with imprisonment in a concentration camp for slander, or even worse, for openly spreading enemy propaganda. If it hadn't been for my father's stepping in to calm things down, there would have been a terrible fight. But thanks to my father's intervention, the argument petered out. The following day Mr. Schröder asked the local Nazi district leader for his views on the subject. And the district leader explained that it couldn't possibly have been the Führer's intention to cast doubt on the virtue of innocent German girls by encouraging the use of reckless slogans.

In the spring of 1943, the Allied air raids on Berlin intensified. We often had to go down to the cellar—which had been reinforced by concrete pillars and served as our air raid shelter—two or three times a night. The Party once again considered evacuating all Berlin schoolchildren. My brother had qualified as a "medic" in the Hitler Youth and was therefore obligated to give first aid in emergencies. As a sixteen-year-old, he now became an antiaircraft helper and was deployed to man the searchlights north of Berlin. Nearly a third of his classmates were killed there during the bombings.[4]

My father, in spite of his bad eyesight, which had so far kept him from military service, was now inducted into the *Landsturm*, the home reserves. He was assigned to guard French and later Soviet prisoners-of-war in Berlin-Staaken. My grandmother, of whom I was especially fond, went to live with one of her sisters in Halbe, south of Berlin. And so my mother and I were by ourselves in the Bingerstrasse apartment. She continued her concerted efforts to keep me from all things coarse and fascist, trying to save me by drawing me into peaceful and "respectable" pursuits, but she was only partially successful. After all, I didn't want to be teased continually by the other boys as a coward or a wimp. I therefore read not only the historical novels or books about animals which, although she could scarcely afford it, my mother bought for me out of her paltry household money—books like *Die gelbe Dogge Senta* (Senta, the yellow Great Dane), *Der Hengst Maestoso Austria* (Stallion Maestoso Austria), and *Abu Markub*—but also the cheap yellow-bordered editions of the War Library for German Youth, which were as popular with boys as Batman or Superman comics decades later.

And that wasn't all. Probably as a protest against my mother's efforts to turn me into a "sissy," I fell in with one of the street gangs that were springing up in our neighborhood. Since almost all the fathers were away at the front and most of the mothers had to work during the day, many children—so-called latchkey kids—were left to their own devices, and gangs were forming all over Berlin in 1942–43. It was clear that many young people were running wild and degenerating into savagery. There were four boys and three girls in my gang. We met secretly in order not to be discovered by the Hitler Youth patrols, who could report us as a threat to the security of the state.[5] Our meeting place was an empty painter's workshop, which we turned into a thieves' den with discarded furniture—worn-out chairs and an old sofa that had been removed from somebody's attic because they would have been a fire hazard if an incendiary bomb had hit the house. And there we pursued all sorts of antiauthoritarian and forbidden activities. We began to smoke, cursed obscenely, and played "doctor" with the girls; we also suspended condoms filled with water from tree branches, and as soon as someone looked up, puzzled to see these things hanging in the trees, we would shoot at the condoms with BB-guns and give the unsuspecting passerby a cold shower. When our leader, Walter, felt especially full of beans, he ordered us to capture other boys or girls and drag them to our den. There he would torment them, sexually and sadistically, taking their clothes off and fiddling around with their private parts. Afterward, with his pants down, he would jerk off under the lustful eyes of Lilo, one of the gang members, just as Big Mahlke did for Tulla Pokriefke in Günter Grass's *Cat and Mouse*.[6]

My mother didn't have the slightest inkling of any of this; had she found out, she would have been very upset. The only thing I did tell her was that my piano teacher was constantly reaching into my pants, whereupon my lessons with this "impertinent lady," as my mother called her, came to an end; nothing further was ever said about it. My mother's main worry was still my speech impediment, which she felt might stand in the way of my chances for social advancement. The neurologist she consulted recommended a therapist, a very successful one, he assured my mother, who treated children by using various kinds of aggressive games in a fascist type of psychoanalysis. At the state's expense Miss Giesecke, who was about thirty years old, had me erect castles with little wooden blocks on the floor, which I then had to destroy, pretending I was in a wild rage. Often she would hit me, throw me to the ground, goading me to defend myself; however, I was rarely able to do so. My mother watched these goings-on with increasing misgivings until one day she finally asked Miss Giesecke to stop her "games" since they weren't having any effect on my stuttering.

The problem of a renewed evacuation of all Berlin schoolchildren became acute at the end of May 1943. The last remnants of the German North Afrika Korps had been captured, the Warsaw Ghetto uprising had been suppressed, Orel had been stormed by the Red Army, and there were more heavy air raids on Berlin, giving the lie to Göring's boast two years earlier that "you could call him Meier" if an Allied airplane were ever to drop another bomb on the city. This time parents had a choice: they could send their children to stay with relatives in rural areas, or entrust them to the KLV.[7] My mother pleaded with me not to put myself into the hands of the Hitler Youth and its KLV organization, but to stay instead with my father's relatives in Hesse. But I was afraid of being with new children who would probably tease me about my stuttering even more than the boys in the Hindenburg school in Wilmersdorf, and so I implored her just as insistently to let me go to camp with my class. When I started to cry, she gave in with a heavy heart.

And so, in June 1943, I again took the train from the Lichtenberg station to the East, unaware of how very much I was going to regret my decision.

THE RENEWED EVACUATION OF MOST CITY CHILDREN

KLV Camp Gross-Ottingen in the Warthegau

June 1943–February 1944

▼

Again we went by train, first to Posen (Poznań), then through Gnesen (Gniezno) to Hohensalza (Inowrocław). From there two buses took us some twelve miles (18 km) in a northeasterly direction to a village called Gross-Ottingen. We never did learn its original name since we were not allowed to have contact with the Poles who lived there.[1] On the bus ride we could see that we were leaving western development behind and entering the more rural eastern area. First, the telephone poles and electric power lines disappeared, and finally the paved roads ended. Gross-Ottingen was a tiny dump comprising fifteen or twenty one-story houses we considered "mud huts," and a red brick schoolhouse that was probably built before 1914. When it rained, the main street dissolved into an impassable field of mud. The village didn't even have a store or a post office.

The schoolhouse had three stories. There were two classrooms on the first floor, which were turned into dormitories for us. On the second floor there was a kitchen, a room for the housekeeper, and a dining room, which also served as a classroom. On the third floor there was another dormitory, two little rooms for the camp squad leader, and a small space used as a smokehouse. During the day, two Polish servant girls worked in the kitchen; they also did our laundry in the cellar. Since the village had no electricity, we usually went to bed with the chickens and got up with them, too. On winter evenings candles were distributed, and later carbide lamps were lit. These gave off considerably more light than the candles but smelled awful. In the nearby barn two long workbenches holding washbasins were set up on the threshing floor. There, every morning after brushing our teeth—something everyone hated—we had to douse ourselves with ice-cold water fetched from a pump in the courtyard between the schoolhouse and the barn. Next to the barn, there was an outhouse divided into four booths. An incredible stench hung over this structure, especially in the summer. A few yards away, wheat and turnip fields began.

After the rain. The main street of Gross-Ottingen (fall 1943). From the author's collection.

There were about fifty boys in the camp, and almost all of us knew one another from the Kirchenpopowo KLV camp. In Berlin, most of us had been in the same class at the Wilmersdorf Hindenburg high school or in the class ahead of mine, and so we were all on familiar terms. Still, there wasn't any real camaraderie. After only a few days—

just as in the first camp—a pecking order was established from which there was no escape. Here too it was the athletic boys, the ones who were physically stronger, the loudmouths, who immediately took over; from the outset the more pampered boys, the weaker ones, or those like me with less self-confidence, didn't have a chance. So I was horrified when my mother came to Gross-Ottingen in August of my first year there and again, unintentionally, made me look like a "mama's boy." Since there was no place for her to stay in the village, she had to get a room in Neu Grabia, a little over a mile (2 km) away. The "facilities" were so primitive there that she left after only four days. As we said good-bye at the Alexandrowo station (today known as Aleksandrów-Kujawki), I implored her not to visit me again; she reluctantly agreed.

The other boys also begged their mothers not to come to Gross-Ottingen under any circumstances. From then on, their letters home contained only positive news about our camp, to make sure that their moms wouldn't even think of coming. But then, they wouldn't have been allowed to write anything negative anyway, since our letters, which had to be very short, were censored.[2] And so our mothers heard only reassuring news from us. And they in turn tried to keep from us any stories of an alarming nature; we therefore knew almost nothing about what was going on in Berlin or in the various theaters of war. Since we had no electricity, there were no radios in camp. I don't remember if there were any newspapers. It is possible that the teachers, the camp director, or the camp squad leader received the *Völkischer Beobachter* (the official Nazi Party newspaper) or the local Warthegau paper, but they never gave us boys a chance to see them. Nowadays nearly every political or wartime occurrence immediately attracts worldwide attention and through television even young people can find out about events all over the world almost as they happen. But in those days, we lived in total isolation. In the fall of 1943, we didn't have the vaguest idea that the Italians had already concluded an armistice agreement with the Allies; that the German army had had to surrender Orel and Smolensk, as well as the Donets River Basin; that in November the aerial bombing attacks on Berlin had started again, heavier than before; that, between December 1941 and January 1944, not far from Gross-Ottingen, 360,000 Poles and Jews were killed in the Kulmhof concentration camp.

Nor were we informed about political events in class. But then, there was no question of regular classes or teaching in this camp. True, we had three teachers. They lived in a house on an estate and came into the camp every morning for two to three hours. But they proved to have little interest in teaching and none in politics. All three were quite unhappy to have been sent to the Warthegau; they saw their transfer as a form of punishment. The oldest was a sixty-year-old math teacher named Meyer, who in addition to algebra and physics taught us some geography. German lessons were given by Mr. Stuller, who was actually an art teacher and who told us he had thought he was coming to a cushy job in Gross-Ottingen. He developed a liking for me and sent my mother—who had made quite an impression on him during her visit—a crayon portrait of me. The third was our old Berlin music teacher Lubczik, who used to scare us because of his bad temper and lack of self-control. He was no more tolerant in Gross-Ottingen, constantly walloping us with a drumstick during the choral singing; he didn't care whether he struck our arms, our backs, or our heads. It infuriated him that since there was neither a piano nor any songbooks in Gross-Ottingen, he had to sing every melody for us so that we could learn it. There were no maps or drawing supplies. There weren't even any books. For more than a year, we had to make do without a single book! The only materials available for classes were pencils, erasers, and notebooks.

But it wasn't just the lack of books and the lackluster teaching—camp conditions as a whole prevented us from learning anything. Although in the fall of 1943 we were already fourth-year high school students (*Untertertianer*), in many subjects we were stuck at a second-year (*Quintaner*), or at most a third-year (*Quartaner*), level. Furthermore, this ignorance was entirely in line with Nazi educational concepts. After all, Hitler never made a secret of how senseless most of the cultural and spiritual values of the "narrow-minded" educated classes seemed to him. He thought "intellectuals" who only had theoretical "knowledge" funneled into them were superfluous. And consequently he thought it was wrong to teach children two foreign languages or to give them specialized training in a field like chemistry. It seemed to him that for a good education that fostered physical hardiness and inner resolution, "a general knowledge" geared to youthful comprehension was quite sufficient.[3] Accordingly, the longer we were in Gross-Ottingen, the less we were burdened with "dead knowledge." Rather, we were provided with sketchy basics, especially in mathematics and spelling. The three teachers, who had shown little interest in camp life from the start, withdrew more and more and left the scheduling of our days to Winter, the camp squad leader appointed by the Hitler Youth.[4]

At first Winter, who was four years older than we were, wasn't all that bad. But after a few weeks, when he didn't meet any resistance, he showed himself a petty tyrant, feared by all the boys. It's possible that there were Hitler Youth leaders who had some feelings of fellowship with those in their charge. But he did not. He used almost every available opportunity to demonstrate his absolute authority. From our first day at camp, he ordered us to wear uniforms and to put our civilian clothes away in the suitcases we had brought or to stow them in the bottoms of our lockers. In addition, he made us get the shortest possible haircuts (probably for fear of lice), though his own hair was considerably longer. In any case, I remember best the long club he carried, a fear-inspiring weapon, and the whistle on a cord around his neck with which he dictated our entire day.

A normal day in Gross-Ottingen went something like this: At 7 A.M. we heard Winter's first shrill whistle, whereupon we immediately got up, ran to the pump in the courtyard, filled the tin bowls that were standing there with water, took them to the barn, and washed ourselves. Then, depending on the time of year, we put on our summer or winter uniforms, made our beds, saw to it that our lockers were shipshape, pulled the windows open to let in fresh air, and swept the floor. The sweeping wasn't easy because we slept on straw-filled sacks that were of a fairly coarse weave, and straw was constantly leaking onto the floor. At 7:45 A.M. there was bunk inspection, for which not only our fingernails and shoes, but also our beds, lockers, and floors had to be in tip-top shape. If Winter found a piece of straw under a bed or a grain of dirt, or if the bedding wasn't precisely squared on the straw sacks, or if the brown shirts in the lockers weren't folded carefully enough, he yelled at us, punched us, or sentenced us to do thirty push-ups. We submitted without protest since we were already used to harsh treatment by our Jungvolk leaders, teachers, and parents.[5]

At 8:00 it was time for the flag-raising ceremony. In the clean-raked courtyard in front of the school, the Swastika would be hoisted. After we all lined up, we had to stretch out our right arm and forcefully recite a morning slogan, ending with the song "Morgenrot, Morgenrot, / Leuchtest mir zum frühen Tod" (Red sunrise, red sunrise, you guide my way to an early death).[6] It wasn't long before we became quite dulled to the emotional excess of this repetitive ritual. Next, jolted into action by Winter's whistle, we marched in double rows up the steps to the dining room. There we stood at our assigned places, forming a large circle with our outstretched arms, and waited, quiet as little mice, until Winter gave the command "Haut!" (Dig!), which we answered with a loud "Rein!" (In!). Then we sat down and ate our thin slices of bread spread with four-fruit jam or artificial honey and drank coffee made from barley malt. At 9 A.M., after we cleared the tables, classes began in the same room and lasted until a little past 12 o'clock. At 12:30, after we had again marched upstairs and bellowed our "Dig in! we were served a one-pot dish or some other modest meal. Sometimes, as a real high point of the day, there might be a sweet cottage cheese dessert. Then there was a brief leisure period, which we rarely knew how to use—aside from playing cards and fooling around. Instead of keeping us meaningfully occupied, for example, by getting us involved in kitchen detail, which would at least have given us the satisfaction of having accomplished something, they left us to our own devices during these hours. The rest of the afternoon was spent— under the direction of the camp squad leader—primarily in sports, singing, field exercises, and marching.[7] In the evening at 6:30, shortly before our sandwich suppers, the Swastika was lowered as part of another hollow emotional ritual. After that, everyone went to bed.

Singing played a central role in all of our activities. Since they had no other instructional materials available and since they couldn't think of anything better, Mr. Lubczik and Winter simply let us bawl out any old folk melodies, soldiers' songs, *Wandervogel* tunes, or Hitler Youth songs. We sang these over and over again, so I still remember more than a hundred of them. I just have to think of the first line and the whole melody comes back to me— along with most of the rest of the lines or even entire stanzas. Actually, I find this quite embarrassing because I now recognize their ideological intent only too clearly. Was I aware of their purpose as a thirteen- or fourteen-year-old? As always, the National Socialists had one simple, irrefutable answer: young people were not supposed to "understand" these songs rationally. Rather, singing them was supposed to "forge young people into a block." Martin Wähler explained in 1934 that the important thing about the Hitler Youth songs was the "rousing mood" that they inspired in ten-to-eighteen-year-olds, a mood which "would only be diminished by explaining the words or subject." Looked at closely, then, these songs appealed primarily to the "heart" and not to the "mind" so despised by Nazi pedagogues.[8]

Fingernail inspection in an Adolf Hitler School (National Socialist propaganda photograph). From H. W. Koch, Hitler Youth: The Duped Generation (New York: Ballantine Books, 1972).

But was this goal actually achieved in camps like the one in Gross-Ottingen? It was for the more robust boys who were enthusiastic about sports and who formed the cadre from which future leaders were supposed to emerge. But how well did it work for the weaker, the less athletic boys, who just let things roll over them in dull and sullen passivity, waiting in hopeless isolation for the end of their suffering? That question is considerably more difficult to answer. After all, even those like me who didn't care for sports still have more than a hundred of these songs rattling around in their heads. And doesn't it therefore seem that the Nazis achieved their goal among the weaker boys too, and that their psychological conditioning of the young people in their power had a formative effect even on the lives of those who found the songs burdensome? At the end of this book, where I consider the aftereffects of the KLV education, I will deal with various aspects of this issue, but I am afraid no clear answer will emerge to the questions raised here.

If memory serves me, we sang primarily fighting and war songs in Gross-Ottingen.[9] Among these, the older marching songs played an important role: "Fridericus Rex, unser König und Herr" (Fridericus Rex, our king and master), "Märkische Heide, märkischer Sand" (The heath and sand of the Brandenburg Mark), "Lippe-Detmold, eine wunderschöne Stadt" (Lippe-Detmold, beautiful city), "Wenn die Soldaten durch die Stadt marschieren" (When the soldiers march through the town), "Es leben die Soldaten / so recht von Gottes Gnaden" (Soldiers live by God's grace), "Kein schön'rer Tod ist in der Welt, / als wer vom Feind erschlagen" (There is no better death in the world than being killed by the enemy), "Ich hatt' einen Kameraden; / einen bess'ren findst du nit" (I had a comrade once; you won't find a better one), "Argonnerwald um Mitternacht" (The Argonne Forest at midnight), and "Wildgänse rauschen durch die Nacht / mit schrillem Schrei nach Norden" (With shrill cries wild geese whir northward through the night). The best known Hitler Youth song was the official march written by Baldur von Schirach, "Marsch der

Hitler-Jugend," which owed its wide circulation primarily to its use as the standard tune for evening entertainments, roll calls, and parades, and also in films like *Hitler-Junge Quex* and *Triumph des Willens* (Triumph of the will).[10] It began with the lines "Vorwärts! Vorwärts! schmettern die hellen Fanfaren. / Vorwärts! Vorwärts! Jugend kennt keine Gefahren. / Deutschland, du wirst leuchtend stehn, / mögen wir auch untergehn," ending with the equally emotional refrain "Unsre Fahne flattert uns voran, / Unsre Fahne ist die neue Zeit, / und die Fahne führt uns in die Ewigkeit! / Ja, die Fahne ist mehr als der Tod" (Forward, forward! the bright trumpets blare. Forward, forward! Youth knows no dangers. Germany, you will be shining bright, even though we may perish. . . . Our flag flutters before us. Our flag represents the new era, and our flag leads us to eternity! Yes, our flag means more to us than death). We also often sang the rather sentimental Storm-trooper song "Als die goldne Abendsonne, / sandte ihren letzten Schein, letzten Schein, / zog ein Regiment von Hitler/in ein kleines Städtchen ei-ei-ein. / Traurig klangen ihre Lieder / durch die stille Stadt, stille Stadt, / denn sie trugen ja zu Grabe / einen Hitler-Kamera-a-ad" (With the last rays, last rays of the golden evening sun, a Hitler regiment marched into a small town. Their songs resounded sadly through the silent town, silent town, for they were carrying a Hitler comrade to his grave).[11]

I remember only one of the songs that were directed against Jews; with the line "Moses, du nimmst ä Bad" (Moses, go take a bath)," it reviled the "dirty" eastern Jews. We sang this song to a melody from Schubert's "Unfinished Symphony"; I was reminded of this in the late seventies during a performance of Heiner Müller's *Die Schlacht* (The battle), in which the same melody served as the perverse background music for Hitler's suicide.[12] On the other hand, we never sang the anti-Semitic songs that Erika Mann mentioned as being typical Hitler Youth songs in her book *Zehn Millionen Kinder: Die Erziehung im Dritten Reich* (Ten million children: Education in the Third Reich) (1938). That also goes for the Nazi agitprop song "Ihr Sturmsoldaten, jung und alt, / nehmt eure Waffen in die Hand, / denn Juden hausen fürchterlich / im deutschen Vaterland" (Storm troopers young and old, take up your weapons, for Jews are wreaking havoc in the German fatherland), as well as the equally bloodcurdling song that appeared in the 1935 volume *Lieder für Landstrasse und Lager* (Songs on the road and in camp) and begins with the verse: "O Herr, schick uns den Moses wieder, / auf dass er seine Glaubensbrüder / heimführe in das gelobte Land. / Lass auch das Meer sich wieder teilen, / wohl in zwei Wassersäulen, / feststehn wie eine Felsenwand. / Wenn das Judenvolk darinne, / wohl in der festen Wasserrinne, / dann mach, o Herr, die Klappe zu / und alle Völker haben Ruh" (O Lord, send Moses down again to lead his people home to their promised land. Let the sea part again into two pillars of water, and when the Jewish people are in the middle of the sea, then, O Lord, let the walls of water close over them, and all people will be at peace). Nor do I remember any of the anti-Bolshevik songs Erika Mann mentions, such as "Du kleiner Tambour, schlage ein! / Nach Moskau wollen wir mar!" (Little drummer, beat your drum! We're going to march to Moscow) and "Hundertzehn Patronen umgehängt, / scharf geladen das Gewehr, / und die Handgranate in der Faust, / Bolschewist, nun komm mal her!" (A hundred and ten cartridges slung over my shoulder, my gun fully loaded, and holding a hand grenade in my fist. Come here, you Bolshevist).[13]

On the other hand, I can't get the haunting tune composed in 1934 by Johannes Scheu out of my head, "Wir lagen vor Madagaskar und hatten die Pest an Bord" (We were lying off Madagascar and the plague was raging on board). It would become our favorite song during the war because of its mindless emotionality, which sucked us in hypnotically. We sang it over and over, not only when we were marching, but also during our time off, because we could so fully, if exaggeratedly, identify with its sentiments. A horde of oppressed pubescent boys, we gradually changed and expanded the words of individual stanzas into macabre and obscene verses, in order to give ourselves release at least on some level. And so in our versions we not only had "putrid water" and the "plague" while lying off Madagascar, but we also had various sailors' brides on board ship, who, just once before we died, would "kiss our stomachs, yes our stomachs." Other songs, such as the ones about the Swabian maidens or the dead girls swimming in a dark canal, were similarly parodied.

We sang most of these songs, even the obscene ones, as we marched on the roads that connected Gross-Ottingen with Klein-Ottingen and Neu Grabia. As part of our physical training, we often had to carry a knapsack and tarpaulins, and as soon as one song was finished, before we had taken ten steps, we had to start a new one. If we couldn't keep in step, couldn't stand the pace, or forgot the words by the time we got to the seventh stanza, we were immediately hounded with commands such as "Auf-nieder" (Up!-down!) or "Zurück, marsch-marsch" (Backward, march! march!). From the very beginning, a rigorous harassment and drill quite in line with the Party doctrine prevailed in this camp. For the slightest violations of camp regulations, we had to report immediately for a "dressing down," and then submit to the prescribed Spartan drill.

It would be euphemistic to call all this training "sports," although we did play Völkerball in the school courtyard in Gross-Ottingen. In these games, just as in Kirchen-popowo, boys like me were again mercilessly chased across the playing field by the more adept athletes. But the martial games had little to do with the pleasure of exercise

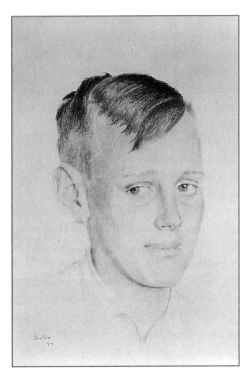

Portrait of Jost Hermand by the drawing instructor Stuller (1944). From the author's collection.

itself. Even the Völkerball games, let alone the marching, the "up-down" drill, and the increasingly rigorous field exercises (sometimes scheduled at night) were designed to prepare us for our later assignments as "soldiers of the Führer." This wasn't sport. It was training for unquestioning obedience, to prepare us for any future action, whatever that might be. As the Nazi pedagogue Max Momsen explained in 1937 in the periodical *Deutsche Volkserziehung* (German people's education), the principal emphasis of physical education of this sort was clearly on the "fighting thoughts" (*Kampfgedanken*), that is, on "man-to-man combat" and the "hardening against pain, the rigors of weather, hunger, and thirst," as well as trust in "the leadership principle" (*Führerprinzip*).[14] As in some of the rural boarding schools that were already being run along fascist principles in 1933,[15] as well as later in the Napolas, Adolf Hitler schools, and Ordensburgen,[16] we boys in the KLV were slated for a "martial" education. In other words, we would be trained first and foremost to be "physically steeled young men."[17]

Consequently, in January 1944, having barely reached my fourteenth year, I had to decide which of the various Hitler Youth groups I wanted to belong to: the aviation group (*Flieger*), the navy (*Marine*), or the signal corps (*Nachrichten*). The air force seemed the most interesting. And so that February, to practice for future responsibilities, I and other classmates who had applied for that group were given a jigsaw, a file, thin plywood, glue, coarse- and fine-grained sandpaper, and instructions on how to build a glider of the "Rhön" class. Since this was our only assignment, I immediately set to work with great zeal. I became even more enthusiastic when I saw how, after I had hoisted it into the wind like a kite on a long string, my "Rhön" sailed over the village and landed in an empty field. But my enthusiasm faded when a group of officers came to our camp to explain the different branches of the service, presenting us with forms to fill out for future voluntary military service. Building model gliders was one thing, but flying a fighter plane against the enemy, even if I were to be awarded the Iron Cross for it, was quite another matter. I am still proud today of what I wrote in my childish script on the form they put in front of me. In answer to the question, "In which of the service branches do you later want to serve your fatherland?" I wrote (because it seemed to me the least dangerous): "As medical orderly with an air force ground crew." I no longer remember how the visiting officers reacted to my entry.

Paramilitary training was the order of the day in Gross-Ottingen during the winter of 1943–44. We received neither formal schooling nor general cultural education. We were merely "toughened up." At the age of fourteen I still didn't know who Goethe and Beethoven were; I had no idea what a poem or a sonata was; and I had only a rudimentary knowledge of history, geography, science, and foreign languages. During these months, we forgot even the little bit of English and Latin we had learned in secondary school in Berlin. The longer we were in the camp, the less we learned about traditional academic subjects. Even worse, no other ideals were instilled in us. Our songs dealt almost exclusively with fighting, willingness to sacrifice, duty, and death for the fatherland, but neither the camp squad leader nor the army officers explained to us the real ideological goals behind these emotional demands for our devotion. The emptiness of the slogans was due largely to the fact that the National Socialists envisioned no "concrete utopia," in Ernst Bloch's sense of the phrase.[18] They were content to rouse the masses, especially the "new young people," for just "any old Third Reich," as Bertolt Brecht had already written in 1932.[19] They didn't want to enlighten their followers or stuff them with facts. Rather, they were primarily trying to charge them up emotionally and at the same time make them physically fit, to transform them into determined fighters who would give their utmost and do "what they were supposed to do."[20]

Thus, from today's perspective, Nazi education is best defined as "shaping young people into a closely knit unit" (*Formationserziehung*) or "attitude training" (*Haltungs-training*).[21] According to the National Socialist catalog of virtues assembled by Hans Friessner, inspector of education and culture of the German army, its prime emphasis was on "healthy ambition, dependability, absolute obedience, a sense of authority, modesty, punctuality, cleanliness, sense of duty, determination, readiness to take on responsibility, toughness, readiness to serve, readiness to sacrifice, discretion, loyalty, incorruptibility, and courage."[22] As Hitler and the Nationalist Socialist education leaders in thrall to him repeatedly stressed, inculcating such values was best done without the influence of the older generation of teachers, who still had not realized that the primary purpose of the new Reich's educational institutions was to steel young people to be fighters, not to impart "dead knowledge."

Jungvolk boys on a cross-country march (National Socialist propaganda photograph). From H. W. Koch, Hitler Youth: The Duped Generation (New York: Ballantine Books, 1972).

And so from the outset, the Nationalist Socialists preferred the camps of the Party organizations to the schools as educational institutions.[23] After 1933, the National Labor Service requirement of working on the land for a year (*Landjahr*), as well as the first KLV evacuations, was clearly set up along the lines of camp education. Students and student teachers were sent to Nazi educational camps shortly after Hitler came to power and—under the new doctrine of physical training—urged to compete for the sports awards presented by the National Socialist Party and the Hitler Youth. The principle of "toughness," that is, of hardening oneself against physical and mental pain, was thus prevalent early on in these camps. Fewer and fewer children, young people, and students were taught by older people. Rather—in the spirit of the National Socialist slogan "Youth educates itself"—they were put in the charge of very young Hitler Youth leaders for this hardness training. It was not the goal of the National Socialists to raise highly educated boys, but to produce exceptionally reliable, competent boys who were ready to sacrifice themselves and who would one day become tough young men, soldiers, or even leaders. Therefore as a rule both the Party leaders and the directors in the early Nazi camps, as well as in the later camps of the KLV, followed Hitler's social Darwinistic concepts. In other words, they did not assign leadership roles to middle-class children; rather, they tried to give opportunities to the disadvantaged boys from whom they expected greater assertiveness and drive. And it worked in some of the camps—especially where the sons of laborers and lower-level office workers predominated. It was in these young people that Hitler placed his greatest hopes since he so despised the "soft" bourgeoisie.[24]

From the start, then, the sociopolitical intention of the National Socialist leadership was neither to preserve the power of the middle class nor to achieve a radical democratization of the German people. To be precise, through its principles of selection, it wanted to start a new class of "young men," men who were ready to fight. In this way, there would always be a supply of dedicated soldiers, as well as proven officers and leaders, for the "great wars" in decades to come. Naturally this did not come off without objections and the compromises of Realpolitik. Hitler made pacts with big industry, the churches, and the Reichswehr, the traditional representatives of the old-guard power structure. However, in education, where in contrast to the higher spheres of society the *real* balance of power was only indirectly involved, he sought to implement his views more forcefully. But here too Hitler knew that a large proportion of the older teachers—out of laziness or political conviction—would slow things down for a while longer. And so he hoped to be able to impose his views on the younger generation through the rigorous training of the Hitler Youth, which led to a marked brutalization in large sections of the educational system. Indeed, in a totally isolated KLV camp like ours, which was mainly in the hands of the Hitler Youth leadership, there was no obstacle to achieving his goal.

There is no doubt that in Gross-Ottingen we were systematically being turned into little savages. The "physical training" that would effect this transformation, because it called forth bellicose behavior, inevitably assumed brutal and violent forms.[25] What began in Kirchenpopowo as games intensified in Gross-Ottingen into the harshest drills and mindless harassment. Even the term *Wehrsport* (paramilitary sports) is too elegant for such methods. The same brutal expectations marked our participation in the 1943 fall harvest, in which the utmost in productivity was demanded of us. In particular, the beet harvest, where we had to cut off leaves for hours on end or push back-breaking loads, proved to be a strain for which we big-city kids were scarcely a match. And yet in all these operations, we tried to do the best we could without groaning or protesting. Even when the local Party farm leader, with whom we normally had little to do, ordered us to chop the heads off chickens, twist the heads off pigeons with our bare hands, or clobber little rabbits behind the ears with a stick and then cut their throats, we did it without blinking an eye. After all, none of us wanted to be called a "sissy."

We passed certain other "tests of courage" with the

same sort of guts. It was considered especially daring to jump down into the schoolyard from a second-story window. It's miraculous that nobody broke a leg in these senseless escapades. When the senior boy in our room ordered us to swallow three live toads, one after the other, we would obey unquestioningly. There were even boys who thought up tests of courage for themselves in order to impress the squad leader, the room senior, or their classmates. I was one of them, and one day I unsheathed the dagger we all wore at our left side and plunged it deep into my right thigh. I still carry the scar. Luckily I didn't injure any tendons with this "manly deed," otherwise I'd be limping today.

Even worse than these tests of courage were the various punishments invented by the camp squad leader who took over after Winter was inducted into the army in March 1944. For one, you might be shut up for several hours in one of the cubicles of the outhouse, unable to sit down or lean against the walls because of the nails protruding from every surface. In the summer, the heat and the stench brought one close to fainting. Or just because you had whispered something to your neighbor at the dining table or had nibbled at your dessert before you were supposed to, you could be locked up in the smoke room in the attic of the school building—a dark cubicle that could only be entered on one's knees and by ducking one's head. Because of the lack of fresh air, you couldn't last more than an hour and a half. To this day, I can't understand why nobody suffocated during this ordeal. But most unpleasant of all was when all the fellows in your room were punished for an offense you had committed. These group punishments consisted mostly of cancelation of free time and a concomitant increase in the marching or harassment drill, that is, the "up-down" exercises. The hardest part wasn't actually the senseless drill, but the contempt,

Physical exercises (National Socialist propaganda photograph). From H. W. Koch, Hitler Youth: The Duped Generation (New York: Ballantine Books, 1972).

the abuse, or the beatings from the other boys that you had to put up with afterward.

Today I think the most reprehensible hardening technique was to teach us to disdain, if not despise, the Poles. Of course, I no longer know precisely how conscious we were of these feelings. Although we realized from our own quasi-military training that the central thrust of National Socialism was aggressivity toward others and constant self-assertion, as thirteen- and fourteen-year-olds we were left in the dark about the ideological underpinnings of Nazism. We merely knew that Reichsgau Wartheland was one of the recently conquered territories. We had no idea of the extent to which the people who had been living in this new *Lebensraum* had to submit to a systematic "Germanization plan" worked out by the Nazi and SS leadership.[26] We did not know that "Polish-ized ethnic Germans" as well as blond and blue-eyed Poles had been designated as "persons who could be Germanized" and that they could apply for German citizenship, whereas Poles who "looked subhuman" were excluded from this privilege.[27] Nor did we realize that the KLV camps themselves were a part of this "Germanization process," which Arthur Greiser, the SS Obergruppenführer and district leader of the Reichsgau Wartheland repeatedly supported in word and deed.[28] I did not find out until long after the end of the war that Hitler wanted to open up a "new settlement area for one hundred million Germanic people" and therefore declared himself opposed to treating the "subhuman" Slavs sympathetically or even decently. Whoever could not be "Germanized," he declared, had to be kept on the lowest educational level, deported, or liquidated.[29]

Since we were not informed about any of these things, we were only superficially aware of the Germanization process. Our KLV camp in Gross-Ottingen, which we were not allowed to leave even once in all those months, was much too isolated for us to get any real insight into prevailing conditions. Consequently, we never found out that there were no longer any Polish schools in this territory, as was also the case in parts of the more easterly and southeasterly Polish territory under German rule;[30] that German had become the only official language in the schools; that as a German you could beat up any Pole as though he were your serf;[31] that all Polish religious services were prohibited; and that what Heinrich Himmler called Polish "parents of good blood"[32] were advised to deliver their children to the appropriate authorities so that they could be transferred to German education camps or Nordic *Lebensborn* (Spring of Life) institutions.[33] Indeed, since all news reports were kept from us, we had not the slightest inkling that this German-ruled Polish territory (the Generalgouvernement) began only six miles (10 km) from our camp, or that there were in that area extermination camps for Poles, Jews, and Gypsies.

I do remember one dreadful occurrence through which we, in the most gruesome way, became aware of the Germanization policy prevailing in the Warthegau. It must have happened in November or December 1943, because it was already very cold. One afternoon we were in the school courtyard when we saw an SS man on a bicycle coming from Standau (Straszewo), his dog running alongside. Because there was so little variety in our bleak schedules, some of us decided to run after him. We saw him suddenly stop and order his German shepherd to jump at a very pregnant Polish woman walking on the village street. The dog obeyed. The woman, probably a maid who worked for one of the German farmers, was very large and already somewhat awkward; with a scream she fell on her back and stared up at the growling dog in great fear. The SS man got off his bicycle and stomped on the woman's belly with his boots until she died from internal injuries.[34]

I no longer remember what went through my mind during this incident, taking place as it did right before our eyes. It was probably a terrible mixture of fear, horror, pity, curiosity, and maybe even lechery, since the woman's skirt had slid up as she fell and her naked legs had come into view. We never asked ourselves why it had happened. We knew only that the woman was unmarried, and so she had committed a "sin." There was no way we could have suspected that she might have been one of those Polish women who according to National Socialist policy were not permitted to reproduce. We thus perceived this scene—which is among the most horrible memories of my early life—not as something political, but rather as vaguely oppressive, and we accepted it fatalistically. In any case, it did not occur to us to rush over to help the woman. I know only that afterward we felt extremely embarrassed and ran back to camp. We never talked about the incident again for fear of coming under suspicion of having been accomplices. We all knew that something dreadful had happened. Yet we weren't able to fit what we had just experienced into our very limited view of life.

We certainly didn't feel that we were members of the German master race,[35] although, in addition to culling out unsuitable Poles, that must have been the intention behind all the toughening, dulling, and brutalizing processes. Most of us felt much too small, weak, and oppressed to identify ourselves with the victors. After all, we also belonged to the less fortunate ones and were bullied in all kinds of ways. Perhaps, if those in charge had treated us more gently, we might have developed the arrogance to look down on the "dirty Poles." But we didn't have this arrogance. We ourselves were part of a pyramidal social hierarchy in which the individual had to assert himself, often quite cruelly, in order to be accepted. There was a clear pecking order among the boys in Gross-Ottingen, as there had been in Kirchenpopowo. And it took a lot of strength and energy to defend the slot you had acquired and to keep from dropping down among the pariahs.

In the winter of 1943–44, our puberty-related cravings for ascendancy, for power over others, became very strong. Especially in the evenings and at night, an aggressiveness prevailed that I am reluctant to describe and can only put into words after making a great effort to overcome my disgust. Again and again things happened during the night which we would consciously minimize during the day, referring to them as *Budenzauber* (dorm parties) or "the appearance of the Holy Ghost." Granted, there were also childish masquerades, in the course of which we slid around on our knees in long processions, mumbling incomprehensible prayers, but almost all our activities ended in violent brawls in which the weaker ones always got the short end of the stick. Looking back on his KLV experiences, Ralf Dahrendorf wrote, "Unfortunately you can't hide the fact that we were not squeamish about how we treated our sensitive, delicate classmates in the camp. To toughen him, anyone who cried could count on being beaten at night by the others in the room."[36]

Even though I never cried or otherwise betrayed my fear, I lived in constant dread of being pulled out of bed by a horde of boys who would beat me to a pulp. So as not to be caught by surprise, I often forced myself to stay awake as long as I could, tossing and turning or pinching my thighs. Not until I heard the regular breathing and snoring of those around me did I finally embrace my pillow and surrender to sleep. Even these tactics were not always successful—because it wasn't just the boys in our room, but sometimes those from the other room who would come to claim a victim to be "slaughtered" on the icy stone floor of the hall. I don't remember our ever going to the assistance of anyone. Each of us was grateful not to be the one being beaten and would rather pull the covers over his head than to let the victim's whimpering "soften" him. Nor do I recall just how often I was the target for these "appearances of the Holy Ghost"; probably not more than four or five times, since from the outset I was considered one of the injured because of my stuttering and so I already belonged among the downtrodden ones. In addition, I tried to get some of the stronger boys to be on my side by helping them with schoolwork or letter writing.[37]

If only these brawls had been the worst of what happened during those nights! Much worse was the sexual sadism, which became more and more relentless with time. "Dorm parties" were the prelude to this torture: the "big guys," the sports aces, would take one of the "delicate and sensitive" boys and strap him down naked on a table. Next he was either smeared with shoe polish and polished with brushes or forcibly masturbated until—after the first climax—he cried out in pain. Other nights the "big guys" would pour lukewarm water on the bellies of sleeping "jellyfish," or "limp dicks," and then, laughing derisively, they would accuse them of bedwetting. And those were the less harmful pranks. Later, as some of the boys had their first ejaculations, and their aroused sexual drive increased, weaker ones, like me, were even raped, and we suffered painful anal bleeding as a result. Over the months, as more boys had ejaculations, the entire ranking system changed. From now on those who could already "come" belonged to the select and tormented the "little boys" in truly mean ways. The showing off of potency became so crass that to demonstrate virility a boy would masturbate in front of the others, catch the semen in a water glass, and then hand it proudly around. There were even contests to measure not only how far one could spit and pee, but also the distance one could ejaculate. The one with the farthest reach was elected "room spritzer."

The big guys weren't the only ones driven by their bodies' physical changes to increased sexual activity; the weaker boys had their problems with puberty too. But they satisfied their urges mostly in secret. Either they masturbated at night under the covers or they had arrangements with other boys, usually those sleeping next to them. Only in the rarest cases did any deeper friendships grow out of these couplings. In Gross-Ottingen even friendship was counted as unfittingly mawkish and soft—and any incipient attachment immediately drew the attention of the stronger boys who would forcefully break it up in order to maintain the existing pecking order.

PREMILITARY TRAINING
SS Ski-training on the Hohe Eule in Silesia
March–April 1944

▼

Unexpectedly, toward the end of February 1944, we learned that we would be going to a ski camp in the Silesian Riesengebirge (the Giant Mountains) at the beginning of March. We were overjoyed. The constant drill in Gross-Ottingen bored us to tears, and all we wanted to do was get away, away from Poland, away from the KLV, and away from the relentless monotony of the camp subordination rituals. We weren't even alarmed when we were told we would be under the supervision of the SS in the ski camp and that it was actually a premilitary training camp.[1] In the first place, we had no idea what SS really stood for, and second, it had been drummed into us not to ask impertinent questions. So we didn't ask what lay in store for us and, resigning ourselves to our fate, blindly hoped for the best. The next few days we talked only about skiing, not about the SS. As Berlin kids we knew nothing about skiing, but we imagined how marvelous it would be to glide effortlessly down long mountain slopes on smooth boards and then soar up the mountain again in chairlifts.

We were all in a great mood on the train ride from Hohensalza (Inowrocław) through Posen (Poznań), Lissa (Leszno), and Breslau (Wrocław) to Waldenburg (Wałbrzych). Even our new camp squad leader seemed a little more "relaxed" that day. He accompanied us as far as Schweidnitz (Świdnica), where he left to go on to a Hitler

Two Hitler Youths skiing downhill (National Socialist propaganda photograph). From Horst Axmann, Kinder werden Pimpfe (Reitlingen: Ensslin and Laiblin, 1938).

Youth training camp. We boys continued our journey toward Waldenburg until we got to a little village in th[e] mountain range called the Eulengebirge (Góry Sowie[)], where two SS officers met our train. The next mornin[g] they took us on a long climb up to the Hohe Eule. On th[e] south side of the mountain, near the peak, was a room[y,] well-furnished mountain hut that must have been one [of] the better establishments of this sort before the war. Fro[m] this hut, at about 3,280 feet (1,000 m) elevation, there w[as] a wonderful panorama of snow-covered mountains. Adult tourists undoubtedly would have stopped to admire the view with "ohs" and "ahs," but we went straight to our rooms to claim the best sleeping spots. The same old rules went into effect on the Hohe Eule—which meant that the weaker boys had to be content with a bed next to the door or in the farthest corner, while the stronger ones secured beds next to a window or the washing facilities.

The two SS officers turned out to be jolly Tirolean mountain guides who had been inducted into the Waffen-SS at the beginning of the war and then transferred into the Mountain-SS because of their professional qualifications.[2] I don't know what sort of ideological training they had had; they kept that to themselves. And so, up on the Hohe Eule, just as in Kirchenpopowo, San Remo, and Gross-Ottingen, there was hardly any talk about politics. Both SS men—being "unheroic" Austrians—were obviously glad they didn't have to fight at the front, happy that they had been posted to this mountain house to give paramilitary training courses to Hitler Youths. They observed the conventions in order not to be considered lenient, but in private they were not as authoritarian as we would have expected German officers to be. On the contrary, after work they would sit for hours with us in the common room, telling us stories of innocent youthful pranks, playing a board game called *Mühle*, or teaching us Tirolean songs we thought were howlingly funny because of their dialect. For their part, the two SS officers found our Berlin accents highly amusing.

This training course was designed for "the purposeful development of soldierly aptitude and knowledge," as stated in a report entitled *About the Condition of Premilitary Training in the Hitler Youth* issued in March 1943 by the inspector of Hitler Youth premilitary training camps, Gerhard Hein. In such courses, Hitler Youths were trained to sharpen their "eyes and ears to meet all possible challenges": they were taught how to use small-caliber guns, to read maps, to carry messages between army units, as well as general "cross-country mobility," as it was called in the jargon of the National Socialist Party. In short, under the general rubric of extensive "field exercises," which went beyond the mere "field games" we had had up to then, these camps were supposed to toughen us "for arduous physical exertions," to "strengthen our will to fight," and to teach us "responsible behavior."[3] On 4 September 1943, "Hitler Youth Premilitary Training Day," Hitler sent a telegram to Reich Youth Leader Artur Axmann about the purpose of these camps: "In the future each new generation in the premilitary training camps will be taught by soldiers who have proved themselves at the front, most of whom were themselves former Hitler Youth leaders. The primary goal of this training is to instill soldierly attitudes and behavior in keeping with National Socialist principles. The soldiers in the front lines expect that now, and in the future too, Hitler Youth will see its highest purpose in this most difficult and fateful struggle to be that of providing the fighting armies with the best new generation of soldiers. National Socialist aspirations and actions must be expressed ever more firmly in the attitude and conduct of our youth. Then they will grow up to be a tough young race that will eventually successfully accomplish all the tasks set for our people by destiny."[4]

Luckily, practice diverged enormously from theory in the camp where we spent March and April 1944. Our days were not nearly so strictly regulated as they had been in Gross-Ottingen. Here we had to endure neither the boring classes nor the torment of cleanliness inspections and flag rituals. True, in the morning we were awakened by a whistle, but after that everything followed a pretty "normal" routine. What we liked most was that we had running water. After we got up, instead of having to get water from the pump and carry it to the barn, we could wash in our own room and even turn on the electric light. Our meals, prepared by a German housekeeper and two young Polish women, were better than in Gross-Ottingen. To get the supplies we needed, we had to hike down to the village every four or five days and carry the foodstuffs in our rucksacks back up to the hut. The road was still iced over, and no car or truck would risk the drive up to the Hohe Eule. I can recall very little else about the daily routine in the mountain hut. However, the many ski exercises, which, after all, were the real purpose of our stay at this camp, stand out more sharply in my memory.

The two SS officers considered the daily ski instruction a toughening-up drill. And even though it was quite strenuous, we enjoyed it. After all, we weren't cruelly berated as in Gross-Ottingen, but rather, in the best sense of the word, we were being trained. As a result, after only a few days we were able to set out on ski tours lasting several hours. These involved more cross-country than downhill skiing. Even today I recall happily the many runs through the fir and spruce forests where, in spite of the lateness of the season, there was still as much as six feet (2 m) of snow on the ground. It may be that I wasn't really aware of the beauty of the landscape but was only astonished at how deep the snow was. We were dazzled by the intensely blue sky and the strength of the sun's rays. Our first morning there—amid much laughter—we smeared our faces with a thick skin cream so that we wouldn't get sunburned. Eventually we recognized the importance of this precaution, which had seemed somewhat "sissy" to us at first. Indeed, in April the sun was so strong that, after lunch—with our arms and chests smeared with cream—we could lie half-naked in reclining chairs in front of the hut.

Although the hut was hooked into the electric network in the valley, we had no radio. But then, this had been the case for a long time, so we didn't miss "the box" at all. We had no idea that during those weeks the Red Army had retaken large parts of the Ukraine, and that the Western Allies, pushing up from the south, were already outside Rome. But even had we known, these battles would have seemed infinitely far away. For boys familiar only with slow trains and even slower buses and still thinking in terms of relatively limited distances, anything that taking place more than 200–250 miles (300–400 km) away might just as well have happened on the other side of the world. Had the war in the East also been an air war, and had we been exposed to bombardment by Soviet planes, the fighting in the Ukraine would surely have seemed closer. But since it was largely a ground war—in contrast to the war in the West, where the civilian population was made aware of the approach of enemy forces through daily raids by Allied bombers—it was much easier to conceal the defeats and shifting front lines.

We were as isolated on top of the Hohe Eule as we had been in Gross-Ottingen. We sang the Hitler Youth songs we had learned, listened to our Tirolean SS officers tell us stories about the pranks of their youth, and in general enjoyed the vast ski world around us. We threw snowballs at one another and laughed at every silly joke without thinking about where we really were. Today I know that the Hohe Eule was only a few miles away from Peterswaldau and Langenbilau, where in 1844, the year of the uprisings by Silesian weavers, there had been bloody disturbances. Our kind but uneducated SS officers had probably never heard of that. And I'm sure they didn't know that Gerhart Hauptmann, the playwright, was working on his Atrides tetralogy just a few miles away in Agnetendorf. In any case, they never talked about any of these things. And although we were already fourteen-year-old high school students and belonged to the young elite of the new Reich, we too gave no thought to history or serious literature.

In the middle of April, we said good-bye to our two SS officers down in the valley and took the local train back to Waldenburg. Many of us felt quite sad. Life had been strenuous up on the Hohe Eule, and the many cross-country ski trips had definitely been premilitary training, but at least we had been treated as boys and could feel enthusiastic about what we were learning. In Gross-Ottingen, on the other hand, we had nothing to look forward to but dreary and uninspiring lessons and the worst sort of harassment drills.

EPIDEMICS
AND THE FIRST PROTESTS
KLV Camp Gross-Ottingen in the Warthegau
April–September 1944

▼

Once back in Gross-Ottingen, we were driven even hard-er than before. The drill whistle shrilled in our ears from morning to night. First we had to get up, go get water from the pump, wash ourselves, and get dressed; next we reported for cleanliness inspection, raised the flag, marched in step up to the dining room, yelled "Dig in!" And so it went, do this, do that, until—an hour after sun-down—we were hounded to sleep by that whistle. And in the ensuing weeks, the "Budenzauber"—for many of the boys the only means of letting off steam to compensate for the increasing pressure exerted on them by the camp lead-ership—assumed really bestial forms. A boy named Gro-towski, who was much stronger than the rest of us, was conspicuous for his brutality during these nightly excesses, which the camp squad leader pretended not to hear. Gro-towski had been transferred to Gross-Ottingen by the Hitler Youth administration as punishment for having set several fires. He had it in for us, and most of the boys in my dorm were scared stiff of him. Not only did he beat us up, but to prove his absolute power over us, he would sex-ually abuse the weaker boys at the height of the nightly escapades.

Probably as a result of instructions our new camp squad leader had received during his Hitler Youth leader-ship course, the paramilitary training was now implemented with a vengeance. In keeping with the Nazi precept "A thoroughly fit, healthy body can't be developed with a short-term course of instruction; it takes constant and regular training,"[1] our marches became longer and longer, and our rucksacks heavier and heavier; the "up-down" drills were extended, so that pretty soon our bodies were hard muscle without an ounce of fat. The field exercises, which were never concluded without the "free-for-all" and merciless "hand-to-hand fighting" demanded by the Party,[2] often began shortly after lunch, so that our leisure time was reduced to a minimum. These exercises wore us out so completely that we would fall into bed some nights too tired even for "Budenzauber."

During these weeks we were also preparing for the National Socialist youth initiation ceremony, which the Nazi Party had copied from the Social Democrats and converted to its own uses. Since one of Hitler's long-term goals was to get rid of all church ritual in Germany and replace it with National Socialist rites,[3] we weren't given a choice in Gross-Ottingen of having a Protestant confirmation or Catholic communion, both of which still existed in the Warthegau. Instead, all KLV boys and girls had to participate in the National Socialist initiation ceremony. For this we had to memorize several pithy sayings about the heroic character of the German people, to be recited in unison or individually. On top of that we also learned several new songs. These included not only Nazi songs about death and resurrection, but also a few operetta and waltz tunes, which our music teacher, Lubczik, who had been enlisted to help with the preparations, liked especially. I'll never forget one of these waltzes, the five-part "Blue Danube Waltz" by Strauss. I was selected to sing the eloquent soprano solo in the second Danube Waltz—"Still ist die Nacht, / die Liebe nur wacht" (Silent is the night, only love is awake). I had become the music teacher's pet while we were practicing this piece, because I was the only one in my class who still had a clear soprano voice. For a while, this kept him from hitting me with the drumstick with which he pitilessly tormented the other boys, most of whom had already dropped down to tenor or bass.

Competitive games for boyish strength (National Socialist propaganda photograph). From Herbert Taege, Über die Zeiten fort: Das Gesicht einer Jugend im Aufgang und Untergang (Lindhorst: Askania, 1979).

As the "big day" of the youth initiation arrived, we marched in our freshly laundered uniforms and gleaming shoes to Standau (Straszewo), a village about four miles (6 km) away, the police and SS headquarters for this district. The ceremony itself was taking place in a big room in an administration building, perhaps the town hall. We were seated in a double row of chairs on the small stage. After we had recited our pithy sayings, one of the SS men gave a short, snappy speech. This was followed by almost an hour of singing. As usual, the first song we sang was the "Horst Wessel Lied," next came "Deutschland, Deutschland über Alles," and then the inevitable "March of the Hitler Youth," which began with the line "Forward, forward! the bright trumpets blare," and then finally the aforementioned "Blue Danube Waltz" series, during which I sweated blood, afraid of missing my entrance cue, although I hoped to shine as a star performer. My short solo went pretty well, but for weeks afterward I had to endure the teasing of the other boys who put me through the wringer because my voice still hadn't changed and I still couldn't "come." Some of them jeered, "You'll never be a man!" Others tried to help me achieve the desired manliness with forced masturbation.

At the beginning of June, I was overjoyed when I was unexpectedly granted two weeks' leave to go back to Germany to stay with my mother. I don't remember how she managed to get me out of Gross-Ottingen, but a few days after the happy news reached me I was sitting on a train going to Posen; from there I went on to Berlin. A Nazi Party decree dealing with the round-the-clock air raids prohibited me from staying with my mother. So the following day, she and I went to Obersuhl via Kassel. Obersuhl is on the border between Hesse and Thuringia. There we were put up by distant relatives in the attic of their old farmhouse; we slept in the same bed. During the next eight days I told my mother, in great detail, all that had happened to me during the last months in camp. I left out only the worst sexual abuse, but I told her everything else we had to endure in the way of "physical training," field exercises, beatings, and punishments. I still remember how upset she was as I told my story, which because of my stutter, I had to start over and over again. She did know, probably from conversations with the people in charge at the Nazi offices where she had applied for my leave, that she could not raise any objections against the customary toughness training and had to be satisfied that I had been allowed to leave the camp for two weeks. And so because she couldn't help me, during those precious days she tried to pamper me in every possible way and to build up my self-confidence.

On the return trip I stayed with her a couple of days in Berlin, in spite of the official prohibition and the continual air raids. Whenever there was an air raid alarm—usually as soon as the early warning signal sounded—she would send me into the coal cellar, where I had to be quiet as a church mouse so that the other residents, who would be coming down to the shelter a short while later led by our air raid warden, wouldn't realize I was there. One night a *Luftmine*, which is what we called blockbuster bombs, exploded about 300 yards from our house. I still remember how guilty my mother felt about having exposed me to such danger. But I tried to calm her as best I could, and the next morning I helped her replace the most critical of the shattered windowpanes with pieces of cardboard carefully cut to fit.

The Jewish family who had lived on the first floor of our house until 1941, and who were not permitted to use the shelter during air raids, were by then no longer there. To this day I wonder why my mother, who was always finding fault with the Nazis, never talked about this. Perhaps the Jewish family had fled Germany—or maybe they had been picked up by the Gestapo. In those years such things happened so clandestinely that only a few people noticed. Most of them were completely preoccupied with their own worries and problems. If my mother had heard anything about the forced deportation of this family, I'm sure she would have been indignant. After all, she never disliked Jews and had always urged me not to let the fascist hatred for them influence me. She said people who enriched themselves with goods left behind by Jewish families who had to leave Berlin after Kristallnacht were "disgraceful egotists."

When I arrived back in Gross-Ottingen at the end of June 1944, I jumped right back into the routine so as not to be thought of as the returning mama's boy. The next two months were among the worst I experienced in this camp.

It wasn't just that we had to endure the martial drill. But because of the appalling hygiene and the deteriorating diet, illnesses were beginning to spread through the camp. The first epidemic was jaundice. Like scurvy, jaundice is caused by a lack of cleanliness and vitamin deficiency. Luckily it didn't last long, because a week after the disease hit, we were given vitamin C pills to take twice a day. We loved to let these pills dissolve on our tongues, just as little Oscar in Günter Grass's *The Tin Drum* did with the sweet lemonade powder. At about this time, a doctor was sent for since a few boys in my dorm room had scabies and all of us were bothered by fleas. He gave us several injections, probably against typhus, and left us some medication for the scabies. The injections he gave us were so powerful that afterward we felt as though we'd been bowled over. We lay in our beds for two days, completely numbed. One of the wise guys said at the time, "Do you know what KLV stands for? *'Kannst langsam verrecken!'* [You can slowly kick the bucket]."

Shortly thereafter furunculosis broke out. Most of us had boils on our arms or legs. At first we didn't know that the little pus-filled boils symptomatic of the disease could become dangerous.[4] We thought the pimples annoying but harmless, sure that they would disappear with time just like adolescent acne, from which quite a few boys in the camp suffered. However, the furuncles did not disappear but multiplied. One of my roommates tried to hide them from the camp squad leader, but that was difficult because our summer uniforms had short pants. Eventually he had more than seventy of these boils on his legs and had to stay in bed because of the pain. At this point, even the healthy and stronger boys stopped laughing at him. Finally, when the sick boy began to groan out loud, we told the camp squad leader. He didn't know what to do either, and thought it would make him look like a worrywart if he called back the doctor who had just given us the injections. So he let the boy go on groaning, bringing him water and something to eat. But two days later when the sick boy became delirious, the squad leader became very concerned. The boy would probably have died had the squad leader not arranged for him to be immediately taken to the hospital.

A boil had developed on my left hand and was rapidly increasing in size. Watching that poor boy whimpering and going crazy with pain, I became terribly afraid, convinced that I was going to die if this boil, which soon extended over my entire lower arm, were to reach my shoulder and the underarm lymph glands. And so in spite of my concerns about being considered a coward, I went to the camp squad leader. I showed him my arm and asked him to take me to see the doctor. Since he couldn't reach the doctor, he sent me to the neighboring village of Neu Grabia, where there was a Polish nurse who worked at a reformatory for young Polish criminals who had raped their sisters or killed their mothers—at least that's what we were told. It was terribly hot that day, but I ran across the fields to Neu Grabia, breaking the rule about never leaving camp alone. When I got there, I found the nurse. She lanced the boil, cleaned the inflamed area, placed an herb compress on it, and wrapped my entire lower arm with two linen bandages. In halting German, she told me to come back in two days.

In bed that evening, it occurred to me that the next time I went to Neu Grabia I could send a letter to my mother telling her about the whole situation, including the infection of my lower arm. Because of my bandaged arm, I didn't have to participate in the camp routine the next afternoon, so I wrote her about all the ordeals we were going through in camp and put the letter in an envelope I had swiped. The next day I went to see the Polish nurse again. She took off the bandages and was pleased to see that the pus was gone. After I thanked her, I begged her for a stamp, pasted it on the envelope addressed to my mother, and dropped the letter into the Neu Grabia mailbox. I had no inkling of the consequences this would have for my mother and for me, indeed, for the entire camp.

When my mother received the letter in which I reported that one of my roommates had nearly died of furunculosis and that I also had a huge boil, she decided then and there to do something about it. Instead of again going to the Schmargendorf Party chapter and applying for special leave for me—which they would surely have denied—she put my letter into her pocketbook, took the next train to Posen, and asked the top Party leaders there for an appointment with Gauleiter Arthur Greiser. This was granted, presumably because such a case had never come up before. She told the Gauleiter about all the severe punishments and rigorous harassment drills I had described to her the previous summer; then she read him the passages from my letter dealing with the outbreak of jaundice and the plague of furunculosis which had almost caused the death of one boy and threatened my own life. The Gauleiter promised that he would immediately send a special Party commission to Gross-Ottingen to check on conditions there. My mother had to content herself with this promise since she had been forbidden to take any other steps, and so she returned to Berlin.

Lo and behold, the Gauleiter kept his word. Only a few days after my mother's appeal, a commission made up of two Party representatives and an army officer arrived in Gross-Ottingen. While the camp squad leader was kept out, they spoke individually and at some length with several boys chosen at random in order to get a detailed picture of the conditions in our camp. With assurance of complete confidentiality, some of the boys leapt at the chance to unburden themselves: they accused the camp squad leader not only of subjecting us to harassment drills and yelling at us but also of locking us up in the outhouse or the smoke chamber for hours at a time, painting for the commission a picture of an absolute reign of terror. One of the Party people even called it a "GPU" system, probably the worst term of political opprobrium imaginable, referring as it did to *Gosudarstwennoyje Politicheskoyje Upravlenie*, the name of the Communist Secret Service until the mid-thirties. After the departure of the commission, our thoroughly confused camp squad leader—luckily he was ignorant of my mother's role in this—tried to impress us with a great show of lenience. But that didn't help him. Ten days later his successor arrived in Gross-Ottingen, bringing with him an order for the old camp squad leader to report immediately to the nearest district military headquarters in Posen to prepare for frontline duty.

The new camp squad leader, who was eighteen years old, wasn't quite as despotic as the previous one; that is, he didn't torment us and shut us into the smoke room. But like his two predecessors he was firmly in favor of unremitting physical training. He had participated in a series of KLV courses where the Party bigwigs had convinced him of the benefits of an education that emphasized "paramilitary toughening-up." He felt it was his primary task to mold us into "truly German young men" by means of brisk roll-calls, extended field exercises, and rigorous team competitions. And our three teachers came to terms with his methods, just as they had accepted those of Winter and his successor. They did their assigned tasks and stayed out of everything else.

We got not only a new camp squad leader in August 1944, but also a nurse. She was given the little upstairs room that had served the former camp squad leader as a living room and which only his favorites had been allowed to enter. The nurse, whose name was Charlotte, was eighteen years old, blond, and well built—in short she was the most beautiful woman we had ever seen. Naturally, she ignited our sexual fantasies. One day after lunch, she unexpectedly stood up in the dining hall and announced that it was her duty to give each one of us a thorough physical examination. The next two afternoons we were to come up to her room one at a time for a checkup. After her announcement, all you could hear in the dining room was apprehensive breathing. We became even more anxious when the camp squad leader got up and instructed us to report for the examination wearing only our gym shorts; we would have to take those off once we were in the nurse's room.

And now something unheard-of happened. Once we were back in our rooms, we decided to disobey the squad leader's order. We who had up to then always followed orders, even in the case of the most brutal punishments, suddenly rebelled. But the only way we could think of to express our defiance was to leave the camp, walk over to a recently mowed field, and swear never to go back unless we were allowed to keep our gym shorts on in the nurse's room. We had endured everything—the smoke room, the outhouse, the "up-down" drills, the beatings, the sexual sadism—but the thought of undressing and possibly having an erection in front of a beautiful young woman terrified us like hellfire. And so there were extended negotiations between the camp squad leader and our room elders, who for the first time stood up to him with a modicum of self-confidence to negotiate a compromise that satisfied both sides. We would be allowed to keep our gym shorts on in the nurse's room, but after that we had to go to the camp squad leader's room for an inspection of our genitalia. And that's what happened. The next two days, one by one, our faces flushed, we went up to see the nurse, who checked our blood pressure and heart rate. Then we went to the camp squad leader's room. After a careful inspection of each boy's penis, he advised us to wash off the "white stuff" under the foreskin every morning to avoid inflammation.

Our insubordination had, for the first time, put in question the absolute leadership principle which had prevailed in the camp. In the next few weeks we were granted more free time and our relations with each other became friendlier. Before, our days had been dominated by merciless drills and our nights by the equally merciless "Budenzauber," leaving practically no room for anything personal. Now we quickly began to develop hobbies and made some tentative friendships. My hobby was keeping animals, which up to that time had been strictly forbidden. Four other boys and I received permission from the camp squad leader to keep some rabbits in homemade wooden boxes, the doors of which were covered with wire netting. We were allowed to set the boxes up in a little shed next to the barn. In addition, I was permitted to keep several pigeons in the loft of the shed. I took a particular fancy to the red- and white-feathered ones. I've forgotten where I got these animals and what I paid for them. Nor do I remember whether I acquired the rabbits and pigeons just because I loved animals or whether I also wanted to fatten them up so that I could slaughter them for my mother in case there was no longer enough food in Berlin. We stole the fodder for our rabbits from the fields at night, mostly beets, grass, or fresh-cut clover. After getting accustomed to their surroundings, the pigeons quickly found their own food, since in the fall there was enough grain in the fields.

The first friend I made was a boy named Sagiraschwili. He was born in Germany in 1930 and spoke the same Berlin dialect as I, but his parents came from the Caucasus region. He was a thin, dark, somewhat reticent Georgian. His father, I later found out, had been a youthful friend of Iosif Dzhugashvili, who had changed his name to Stalin in 1917. My friend's father renounced Communism in the twenties and became a leading member, if not in fact the commander, of a Georgian resistance group supporting a "Free Georgia." After an unsuccessful uprising, he was captured by the Red Army in 1927, taken to Moscow, and condemned to death. However, in response to protests from the German high command, he was pardoned by Stalin and deported to Germany. There, sometime after 1933, he joined Rosenberg's staff, and during the last years of the war was one of the political commissars of the Nazi-organized Wlassow Army composed of captured Ukrainians and Georgians. However, the Nazis were profoundly distrustful of the true intentions of these troops and never sent them to fight on the eastern front.[5] The young Sagiraschwili knew no more about all this than I did. In any case, I don't remember ever having talked about politics with him. Our primary bond was that we both felt we were outsiders. And so we were glad when, after making several swaps, we were able to sleep in adjoining beds. Our liking for each other developed into a genuine friendship.

We had no idea what was happening in the various theaters of war at this time. Nevertheless, as our teachers and camp squad leader became increasingly tense and nervous, it began to dawn on us that things didn't look good for the Germans. By August and September 1944, German resistance was weakening on all fronts. In Italy, the Allies had reached Tuscany. The long-planned Allied invasion had taken place in France. Indeed, on 25 August, the Allies were already entering Paris, and on 11 September, having taken northern France and Belgium, they reached the German border. At the same time, German troops were forced to withdraw from Greece and Finland. Germany also had to deploy special units to put down uprisings in Warsaw and Slovakia. During those weeks the Red Army seized Transylvania, advanced toward Yugoslavia, and reached the Czechoslovak border.

Yet in Gross-Ottingen our routine continued as though nothing had changed: every morning we reported for cleanliness inspection, marched two by two up to the dining room, learned to sing new Hitler Youth songs, and went out into the fields at night to steal food for our bunny rabbits. But gradually a sense of foreboding overtook us: something dire was happening and whatever it was might have consequences for us. And so we were not surprised when at the end of September we were informed that our camp was to be broken up. However, we were not told why. We weren't even told where we were going. Many of us hoped we would finally be allowed to return to Berlin, but this was not to be. As we were boarding the train in Hohensalza—carrying our battered suitcases as well as our rabbit boxes and pigeon baskets—we found out that the KLV administration was sending us to a new camp in Sulmierschütz near the Silesian border. Many of the boys were crestfallen at this news. Some, and I was among them, angrily threw parts of our uniforms out the train compartment windows and put on the civilian clothes that had been packed away in suitcases and lockers for more than a year. Our disappointment was so great that we no longer sang "Forward, forward! the bright trumpets blare. Youth knows no danger," but only "We were lying off Madagascar and the plague was raging on board."

THE LAST STAND
KLV Camp Sulmierschütz in the Warthegau

October 1944–January 1945

▼

This time the train went via Posen (Poznań) to Lissa (Leszno) and then on to Krotoschin (Krotoszyn). From there we were taken in two buses to Sulmierschütz (Sulmierzyce). The camp squad leader was in charge. Our three teachers, the housekeeper, and the nurse remained in Gross-Ottingen to await transfer to another camp. Two new teachers, Dr. Krohn and Dr. Hilpert, were waiting for us in Sulmierschütz. Dr. Hilpert was a brother of the famous director, Heinz Hilpert. Neither he nor Dr. Krohn had any previous KLV-camp experience. They were horrified when they saw us pour out of the buses wearing casual clothes and unloading rabbit boxes, pigeon baskets, and sacks of animal feed. They had expected secondary school boys from Berlin—the young elite of the nation. Instead they were faced with a horde of half-grown barbarians yelling at the top of their lungs and then immediately falling into line when the camp squad leader blew his whistle. So, instead of greeting us with some well-chosen words and escorting us into camp, they left us hooligans to our leader, and stepped aside in hapless bewilderment.

I liked Sulmierschütz on first sight. It was a little town of about fifteen thousand inhabitants, most of them Poles. In the center, there was a city hall in the middle of the market square, just as in Posen and other towns in the area. The main streets were paved, and there were telephone poles and electric power lines. We were most impressed.

Accustomed to plodding through mud and making do with candles and carbide lamps, we looked forward to the luxury that awaited us here. And we didn't have long to wait. Our new home, the multistory schoolhouse that stood next to the church, had electric lights, running water, and even toilets that worked passably well. Moreover, we weren't crammed into just two sleeping areas. Instead, there were four rooms at our disposal, twelve boys in each. But we were immediately faced with a problem in this small town: What to do with our animals? Ever resourceful, we discovered a small bakery with a little barn and a cowshed across from the school. The owner gave us permission to keep our rabbits in the loft of his barn and even to "habituate" the pigeons there.

Today it seems to me incomprehensible that they should have tried to set up a new home base for us in the southern Warthegau at the beginning of October 1944—just as the Allies were capturing Aachen and the Red Army was advancing on East Prussia. The Wehrmacht—by now fighting on German soil and surrounded on all sides—was suffering one defeat after the other, while we were still sitting in what was once Poland. Dr. Krohn assured us that the apparent setbacks—which we were gradually getting wind of—would one day lead to the victories we'd become accustomed to expect. In a speech on 9 November (the anniversary of Hitler's 1923 Munich coup attempt), Dr. Krohn explained to us that he based his hopes primarily on the V-3, the miracle weapon with which Hitler was expecting to effect a turnaround in the war. As the director of our school, Dr. Krohn was a Party member, but he was more a follower than a fanatic. He never went as far as Reich Youth Leader Artur Axmann, who wrote about the deployment of German youth in the *Völkischer Beobachter* of 3 September 1944. In the article, entitled "Nazis Through and Through," he declares: "As the sixth year of war begins, Adolf Hitler's youth stands prepared to fight resolutely and with dedication for the freedom of their lives and their future. We say to them: 'You must decide whether you want to be the last of an unworthy race despised by future generations, or whether you want to be part of a new time, marvelous beyond all imagination.'"[1]

Two passport pictures of Jost Hermand (spring 1940 and fall 1944). From the author's collection.

When my mother heard that we had been shipped to Sulmierschütz, she went to Breslau (Wrocław) and somehow managed to get permission for me to visit her there for three days toward the end of October. Since the political situation had worsened dramatically by then, I was less afraid of being teased about such a trip by the others. More than likely, they envied me for once again getting permission to leave the camp.

I wish I could remember more clearly the days I spent in Breslau. I recall only that my mother and I stayed in a small hotel, a relatively peaceful place, since Breslau had so far not suffered any air raids. My mother took the opportunity to buy me my first real suit—replete with knickerbockers—to make a "young man" out of me. To commemorate this "historic moment," I had to sit in a photomat and have some pictures taken while wearing the new suit. On our last evening together we went to the circus because—given my great love of animals—I wanted, finally, to see some live lions, tigers, and elephants. That evening I also asked my mother to tell me all about Tinga, the dachshund she had bought for me in the spring of 1943.

The things she told me about Berlin were quite disheartening. Mother was depressed not only by the increasing frequency of the air raids, but also because the Party "had it in for her." Most of all, Mrs. Krautwurst, the official Party block warden who was inspired by a mystical love for Hitler, kept harassing her, harping on the fact that my mother never gave more than fifty pfennig when she came around to collect for the National Socialist Party, Winter Relief, the Organization of Germans Abroad, National Socialist Peoples Welfare, and similar organizations—instead of contributing five marks the way "a good German" should. And then, on top of that, Mrs. Krautwurst also remembered that I had once made a very impudent, although childishly innocent remark. This had happened back in the spring of 1943 during a campaign to "fight spoilage." Twice a week, I had been ordered to take the heavy and stinking trash cans filled with vegetable garbage from our house to a designated place where it was being collected for animal feed, and I had said to Mrs. Krautwurst that I didn't want to have anything to do with "Nazi swine."[2] Naturally, she blamed my sullen, thoughtless words on my mother's refractory character. Let's face it, my mother was a thorn in Mrs. Krautwurst's side because she was pretty.

Thus, in early October, as had happened after her trip to Posen, my mother was summoned to the Schmargendorf Party chapter. There she was sharply reprimanded for never saying "Heil Hitler" on the stairway of our house or in the stores on our street, for not contributing enough money to the Party, and for exerting an influence on me that "threatened the security of the state"—all of this according to "reliable testimony." To avoid being put in prison, my mother replied that the name of the Führer was much too "sacred" to her to be repeated constantly. Luckily they found this convincing. Her answers to the other accusations weren't quite as quick-witted. And so the following week she was ordered to sew uniforms ten hours a day—a chore she was able to perform for a while in a factory and then as piecework at home.

During November and December 1944, we received the most regular classroom instruction we had had in any of the KLV camps. Each teacher, in his own way, tried very hard to plug at least some of the gaping holes in our knowledge. I remember best Dr. Hilpert's German literature classes in which I learned about Goethe, Schiller, and Kleist for the first time. I still recall listening to him, hanging on his every word as if mesmerized. He recited certain dramatic scenes with terrific panache and expressiveness. And the more sensitive and more responsive of us—even if we didn't understand the substance of the work—were transported to another world of which we had had no previous inkling. To this day, some of these recitations echo in my head, for instance, the final scene from *Egmont*, the Rütli oath from *William Tell*, and the *Prayer of Zoroaster* by Kleist. In contrast, I only vaguely recall the voice of our camp squad leader, who continued to make us march and sing during those weeks, although we were no longer in uniform and the morning flag drill had been dropped. Dr. Hilpert, who was not a fascist and perhaps was even antifascist, had a lot to do with the increasingly critical view of the Hitler Youth on the part of the bigger boys and star athletes, who were also beginning to see through Dr. Krohn's grand hopes for the V-3, realizing this was mere propaganda.

The many ethnic German groups who were funneled into the Warthegau from the East between 1939 and 1944 in accordance with the resettlement policy imposed by the SS played an important role in our heightened awareness of the situation. During that time, 135,000 so-called ethnic Germans were "transferred" to this territory from Galicia. In addition, there were 28,000 from eastern Poland; 49,000 from Estonia; 50,000 from Latvia; 93,000 from Bessarabia; 97,000 from Bukovina; 11,000 from the Caucasus; 72,000 from the Ukraine; 73,000 from the Black Sea region; and 45,000 from East Volhynia, in the Ukraine.[3] The resettled people we met in Sulmierschütz were almost all Black Sea Germans, who arrived with their families, in a long train of canvas-covered horse-drawn wagons, in the fall of 1944. In order to further "Germanize" the Warthegau, the SS authorities were to see to it that they were resettled in the area between Ostrowo (Ostrów Wielkopolski) and Kroto-schin (Krotoszyn). Many of those arriving were descen-dants of Swabians who had been given large estates in southern Russia by the Empress Catherine in the eigh-

Germans from the Soviet Union arriving in the Warthegau (1942). From Deutscher Osten. Land der Zukunft, ed. Heinrich Hoffmann (Munich: Heinrich Hoffmann Verlag, 1942).

teenth century. With time they had become respected wine growers and champagne makers who were permitted to hold on to their farms and wine cellars as private property, even under Stalin. We were surprised to hear some of these farmers, still using their Swabian dialect, speak lovingly of "Papa Stalin," who had pinned prestigious medals on their chests in the Kremlin, honoring them for being "activists" or even "heroes of labor." They kept the medals in little red-and-gold boxes, proudly showing them off to everyone. These Black Sea Germans were extremely bitter about being forced to give up their farms by the SS and compelled to trek westward when the German army retreated. The "worthless sandy Polish soil," as they called it, seemed a poor substitute for the fertile farmsteads of their homeland. So they grumbled incessantly and made no secret of their antipathy toward the Nazis.

A combination of factors, including our getting to know the Black Sea Germans, Dr. Hilpert's influence on us, as well as the overall political situation, finally led to our camp squad leader losing his authority in December 1944. Up to that point, with the exception of the incident sparked by the nurse and the physical examinations, we had obeyed even the most absurd commands of our Hitler Youth leaders without protest. Now, however, there was an increasingly stubborn opposition to all orders coming from "on high." Just the fact that we no longer wore our uniforms and had let our hair grow longer had given us a new feeling of self-worth. Suddenly we ceased being crew-cut Hitler boys who would spinelessly let themselves be drilled and tormented. We were now young men, toughened by many months of paramilitary exercises, who wouldn't be pushed around. Over the years, we had not only learned to obey our leaders but also, following the rule of the jungle, to assert ourselves ruthlessly against all comers.

These changes were reflected in what we did with our spare time. Before, we had submitted completely to the orders of our camp squad leader. Now, in our free time, we began to develop our own activities. A few of us worked part time in the largest of the town's bakeries because there was always something one could nibble on. Others, including me, worked for farmers in exchange for fodder for our animals. During those weeks there was also a lot of work to be done in the camp. Because of intermittent interruptions in the electric service, we'd have no running water, so that we would suddenly be dependent on the pump in the marketplace. But what I liked most during those weeks, before it got too cold, was to go up to the shed loft with a few of my roommates. There, we would do the usual "hand jobs," and when I "came" for the first time, there was great jubilation. Other times we played cards or just talked.

In this new ambience of freedom, my roommate "Kutzi" and I decided, in violation of the rules, to simply leave the camp for a few days and go to Berlin to see our parents. We informed the camp squad leader of our intention; he gave in and merely asked us to come back as quickly as possible. Since we didn't want to arrive in Berlin empty-handed, we killed our rabbits, skinned them, tossed them into our backpacks, and marched off in the direction of the depot in Krotoschin. After a long wait there, we finally boarded a train, only to become scared at our own daring. We tried to bolster our courage by singing some of the marching songs we had learned.

When we arrived in Berlin, an air raid alarm was in progress, but it lasted only an hour so that we were able to run home that same evening through the dark streets full of rubble and destruction. I already knew that after an especially massive air raid only the firewalls and the front facade of our house on Bingerstrasse were still standing.

My mother had escaped death in the air raid shelter. So I ran to Rüdesheimer Platz where my parents' closest friends lived; they would be able to tell me where she was now staying.

Even before I rang the bell, I heard my mother's voice inside, and I couldn't contain myself for joy. She was just as happy as I when she opened the door a moment later. Not only my mother and her friends were in the apartment; my father, whom I hadn't seen for a long time, was there too. He had been guarding French and Soviet prisoners of war; then, in 1943, in Straussberg near Berlin, he managed to get a discharge from the army because of his weak eyes. After that he had worked for a textile firm which also ran several factories in the Ukraine. Twice his firm had sent him to Kiev and Vinnitsa for several months to help supervise production there. He didn't like to talk about the business part, preferring to tell about the jolly evenings he had spent there, entertained by Ukrainian folk singers and dancers.

Meanwhile, however, his relationship with my mother had worsened considerably. A resentful lower-middle-class husband, he wanted to show his opposition to her antifascist leanings and had joined the Nazi Party just a short time before. And so the next few days were not quite as harmonious as one might have expected for a family reunited after a long separation. My mother spent most of the time at her sewing machine so as not to get behind on her uniform piecework, while my father devoted himself to the bottle. I was glad to return to camp shortly before the New Year.

During the following weeks, the situation in Sulmierschütz became more tense by the day, even though our teachers did everything they could to lend camp life a certain degree of stability through regular classroom instruction. In addition, Dr. Krohn tried desperately to boost our spirits with the usual die-hard slogans and hints that the V-3 rocket was now operational and would win the war for the Germans. But we had heard this so often, we knew it for a cliché.

Two factors in particular made us apprehensive. First, we could see that the Poles were getting more rebellious. To prevent an open uprising, the German authorities finally ordered a curfew between 6 P.M. and 7 A.M. and forbade the gathering of large groups during the daytime. Anyone who violated these rules was mowed down by the machine guns of an SS unit that had taken up position in the market square. Second, we had started listening secretly to enemy radio broadcasts at night, especially the BBC's programs for German listeners called *Für deutsche Hörer*, which was introduced by the first measures of Beethoven's Fifth Symphony. After the electricity broke down, we improvised, using a crystal, a detector, a wire hidden behind our lockers, a battery, and earphones to receive these broadcasts. We heard that the Red Army had taken Warsaw on 17 January and at the same time was pushing forward into the industrial area of Upper Silesia. This put our camp very close to the front lines.[4]

Dr. Krohn tried to screen himself from such reports as long as possible, continuing to place his hopes in the V-3. And our camp squad leader tried to keep up our spirits with the old standby Madagascar song and another which started with the words: "Das kann doch einen Seemann nicht erschüttern" (Things like that can't shock a sailor).

But one morning it happened. Although the evening before we had to listen to a calculatedly reassuring talk by Camp Director Krohn, that morning after breakfast—probably on orders from above—he told us to drop everything and march with him to Krotoschin. We were quite willing to leave behind the few personal things we owned. But we knew that the distance to Krotoschin was more than ten miles (15 km) and that it was bitterly cold outside. Experienced survival artists that we were, we each put on two additional sweaters and stormed into the kitchen to supply ourselves with the necessary provisions. After a cursory inspection of the inventory, three of us decided to fill a lightweight pail with oatmeal, sugar, and cocoa, so we'd have something nourishing to take along on our march.

We weren't the only ones on the endless road to Krotoschin that day. Other Germans, especially the Black Sea farmers, were converging on Krotoschin, where the last train to the West stood waiting in the station. Knowing that those who didn't reach the train in time would either be killed by the Poles or end up as Soviet prisoners, the farmers were doing their utmost to get to the train depot. Although one farm family who had come from far away in an open wagon, and whose newborn child had died from the cold during the journey, allowed us to suspend our increasingly heavy pail on one of the wooden poles projecting from their wagon, little solidarity prevailed among the fleeing Germans. Everyone tried to move as quickly as possible so as to reach the train that would carry them to safety. Some probably were glad that others lagged behind and that they could be at the front of this miserable procession.

When we arrived in Krotoschin, there was the train. It had two locomotives and about twenty-five cars that were already quite full. Still, the three of us succeeded in pushing our way into a partially occupied compartment. The train wasn't scheduled to leave until evening, and new refugees were continually streaming into the station. By early afternoon most of the cars were so full, you could hardly move. There were at least twelve people in each compartment, and many were standing in the corridors, so it would have been unthinkable to leave one's seat. But it wasn't just the people. Baggage, baby carriages, and piles of suitcases belonging to those who had come with hand carts or horse carts were stacked everywhere. The carts—horses and all— were abandoned outside the station. Some of the late arrivals smashed the train windows from the outside, pulled pieces of baggage out of the corridors, and threw them onto the platform. The owners protested vociferously. It wasn't until we heard the chattering of distant machine-gun fire that this uproar let up. Everybody was glad just to be standing, squatting, or sitting somewhere on the train—even without their possessions. At least they could save their skins. In the light cast by lamps on the station platform, we could see still more Germans arriving as the train pulled out. They remained behind, soon to be engulfed by the battles that broke out between rebelling Poles and German army units fighting for their lives. Many of the escaping Germans probably didn't survive the next few days.

The train went by way of Lissa (Leszno), Glogau (Głogów), Grünberg (Zielona Góra), Guben, and Cottbus to Berlin. The trip took more than forty-eight hours since we had to make many stops while barriers on the tracks and other obstacles were removed. The first night was especially bad. Nobody could leave the compartments because the corridors were full of people. It was icy cold. If you had to "go," you had to stick your naked bottom out the window. The rest of the time, we pressed as close to one another as we could so as not to freeze in the unheated compartments. I was fortunate in that I was sitting on a narrow bench next to a plump elderly farm woman from the Crimea. She radiated lots of body heat and put her motherly arm around me. When we arrived in Glogau on the second afternoon, we were allowed to leave the train for the first time. But practically no one did, afraid of losing the places they had fought so hard for. We three boys just asked people on the platform to hand us something warm to drink through the window—it was probably barley-malt coffee—and fed ourselves from what was left in our oatmeal pail. The Black Sea farmers, who felt it was all over now anyway, gave us a big piece of their homemade sausage.

Toward the end of the third day, we arrived at the Silesia

station in Berlin. With our wrinkled coats and unwashed faces marked by the rigors of the journey, we must have looked like thugs. And that's how we felt too. In any case, we were in no mood to ever again be ordered around by hysterical political idealists. On the dark platform we bumped into a group of Hitler Youth leaders and Party bigwigs who wanted to send us to a new camp in Pomerania. They explained that there was a train on the next platform which would take all the boys from Sulmierschütz to this camp. But we just sneaked away from them, mingling with the other refugees, and then we ran as fast as we could through the gate. I don't know how long it took me that evening to walk from the Silesia station to Rüdesheimer Platz. It was after midnight when I rang the bell. After a little while, my sleepy-eyed mother, an overcoat thrown around her shoulders, opened the door. At first she didn't realize that the half-frozen, dirty young man standing in the doorway was her son. But when she recognized me, she took me in her arms. I was home again, at last.

RETURN AND READJUSTMENT
Rauischholzhausen and Kassel
March 1945–March 1950

▼

Our apartment on Rüdesheimer Square was anything but
a safe harbor. In the weeks that followed, we often had to
spend hours at a time in the cellar shelter, not only at night
but even during the bright daylight hours. All around us
bombs were exploding, each blast preceded by an eerie
whistling noise. During those moments my mother often
covered me with her body, as though she could in this way
protect me from danger. Under the circumstances, there
could be no thought of attending school or renewing con-
tacts with my old classmates. Almost everyone was waiting for it all to end—either in total destruction, or, possibly,
survival. My brother was stationed at the western front,
and my father had been called up at the last minute to serve
in the *Volkssturm*, the last conscription. Consequently,
toward the end of February, my mother felt there was no
reason to keep sewing uniforms for the Party. To escape
the relentless air raids and the approaching Red Army, she
decided to flee to the West with me. I can still see us,
boarding one of the overcrowded trains in the half-
destroyed Potsdam station. There had been a devastating
daytime attack by an American bomber squadron, and
enormous fires were burning everywhere. I remember how
indignant some of our fellow passengers were when they
noticed that I was carrying my dachshund, Tinga, in my
hand luggage—how terribly inappropriate and sentimental

amid the universal human suffering and hunger. One of them sniffed that a dog like Tinga would make a "good breakfast."

After arriving in Marburg, we took a bus to Rauisch-holzhausen in the Ebsdorfer Valley. We had come here to look up relatives of the family that had sheltered my mother in their Rüdesheimer Platz apartment after she was bombed out of her place on Bingerstrasse. The relatives, whose name was Kaiser, had a beautiful house and farmstead in the village. After the bleak years I had spent in the Warthegau, it looked like a palace. I was profoundly impressed by the half-timbered construction, the carved wooden stairway, the six horses, the thirty cows, the tractor, and the electric milking operation. And so I didn't mind at all when Mr. Kaiser, whose only son had been killed on the eastern front, hired me as a farmhand. That meant I had to get up at five o'clock every morning. First I helped a Polish worker muck out the horse stalls, and then for the rest of the day I worked in the fields. Soon, after only a little instruction, I was allowed to drive the tractor, to plow and harrow; such things were expected of a fifteen-year-old boy in that region.

Although I don't remember much about the specifics of the farmwork, I remember the end of the war down to the last detail. The news reached Rauischholzhausen toward the end of March. One day we heard that the Americans had entered Marburg and that they would certainly also pass through our village. That evening, after dark, my father turned up unexpectedly. He had taken an army bicycle after deserting the Volkssturm in Lich, where he had been an office worker. Now he wanted to get rid of his uniform as quickly as possible. Mr. Kaiser, who had not been a Nazi Party member but had served as an elected representative of the German Democratic Party in the Prussian legislature before 1933,[1] quickly gave him some civilian clothes and buried the telltale uniform behind the barn. The following day he introduced my father to Mrs. Kaiser and the farmhands and servants, saying that he had just arrived from Berlin. That morning I had to plow a distant field with the two mares, Frieda and Bertha, my favorites. Toward noon, I saw an American tank take up a position on a nearby hill and fire some warning shots in the direction of Wittelsberg, Rossdorf, and Rauischholzhausen to let the inhabitants of the area know that the Allies were now the new masters. The horses and I stood still for about five minutes as the shots rang out. Then I watched the tank disappear from sight and, unfazed, continued with my plowing.

In the next few days, not much changed in the village except for the appearance of a notice that said that anyone hiding a German army deserter would be severely punished. But Mr. Kaiser ignored the warning and did not turn my father in. Nevertheless, the situation made my father extremely uneasy, and a few days later he rode off to Kassel on his bicycle to look for a job. Because he claimed that he wasn't politically "handicapped" by having belonged to any of the National Socialist organizations, and also because his passport said "Former citizen of the U.S.A.,"[2] the American occupation authorities gave him a managerial job shortly after his arrival in Kassel, and later made him director of a factory there. With this unexpected improvement in his fortunes, he immediately sent for my mother. However, since Kassel had been almost completely destroyed and he could find nothing better than a little attic room as temporary lodgings, I stayed behind in Rauischholzhausen, where I was now officially an "agricultural trainee." In early May, the two Polish farmworkers, who had been treated decently by Mr. Kaiser during the war, left with generous pay and sufficient food for the road. They were heading for Stadtallendorf, where the

American military authorities had set up a collection camp for eastern Europeans who wanted to return to their homes. Now I was promoted, perforce, to second in command on the farm, and I thought that this would mean the beginning of a completely new life for me.

But my experiences of the KLV and the Third Reich that produced them were not to be put out of mind as easily as I had hoped in the spring of 1945.[3] One couldn't just start from zero. Although in the next few months I worked to exhaustion in Mr. Kaiser's fields from early morning till late in the evening, the experiences I had had in the various camps and in the Hitler Youth haunted me incessantly. I don't mean this just generally, in the sense that all our accumulated experiences become part of us and thus continue to affect us subconsciously even as they seem to fade from memory.[4] Rather, I couldn't come to terms with the details of my KLV experience, and I must admit that in Rauischholzhausen I had no chance to bring even temporary order to the chaos of my contradictory feelings. In the first place, I was still much too young for real understanding. Second, the demanding physical labor left no time for reflection; at night I would fall into bed completely worn out. And third, nobody in the village would talk to me about fascism. The only political subject they would sometimes touch on was the war. But even these conversations were usually confined to personal experiences and did not touch on the big questions of right and wrong.

How could I know then which of my KLV experiences to consider beneficial and which detrimental. Even a few years later when I began to reflect with more awareness about the years before 1945, I was often not sure whether only good things produce good results, or whether sometimes bad experiences can also result in some good. It wasn't until much later that I realized how many of my actions and decisions right after the war, especially during my stay in Rauischholzhausen, were directly or indirectly connected with the KLV experiences described in this book—either as already established compulsions or as reactions to such neurotic behaviors.

In looking back, I have become increasingly aware of how hard it is to distinguish between individual and collective experiences. And at the same time, I realize how tempting it is to indulge in wild speculation in the course of arriving at a psychological interpretation of political processes. I know from conversations with other people, especially with victims of the Nazis, that they too sometimes ask themselves whether it wasn't the awful and life-threatening experiences they had in prisons or concentration camps that strengthened their will to survive.

Perhaps I should be thankful to the KLV for its brutal lessons in survival. Certainly I could scarcely have endured the terror and epidemics in Gross-Ottingen if I had not learned to be self-reliant. I probably would not have developed the fortitude that life demands if I had grown up in Berlin in the sole care of my mother and sympathetic teachers like Dr. Fette. Chances are I would have remained a sweet but weak personality. In a society that is in the fullest sense enlightened, peaceful, and based on solidarity—in short, a deeply humane society—the gentle upbringing and education that nurtures sensitive and handicapped children would doubtless be the proper prerequisites for a happy adult life. But there has never been such a society—and I am afraid there never will be. In all competitive societies—whether middle class and liberal, capitalist, or fascist—only the disadvantaged or disabled who are able to assert themselves forcefully manage to secure a place in the sun next to those who have been favored by birth and natural ability. And so, perhaps the merciless training in the KLV camps kept me, a timid, stuttering child of the lower class, from becoming a "weakling" and a failure in the eyes of society today.

Thus, in spite of my Berlin dialect, which the villagers

found comical, in spite of my speech defect, my big-city background, and my limited physical strength, I had no problem in becoming "crown prince" in Rauisch-holzhausen. By the same token, none of the work there seemed too difficult, whether it was plowing, mowing, binding sheaves of wheat, harvesting potatoes, mucking-out, threshing, or chopping wood. Only once did I come close to failing. I had to pile a load of wet beech logs on a wagon. Although the task called for far more strength than I possessed, I did not give in. And when I had finished, I proudly drove the wagon piled high with wood back down the hill. And while I was very fond of animals, I did every-thing that was expected of me without any squeamishness. Not only did I feed them, give them water, and groom them, I also helped out with castration of a newborn foal; saw to it that the bull mounted the cows; helped pull on a leather thong in the middle of the night, dragging calves out of laboring cows; and when a pig was slaughtered, I held the bowl to catch the gushing blood. Like other peo-ple raised on a farm, I considered these hard and brutal things to be quite natural.

In addition to fortitude and the ability to assert myself, I also attribute my unsociability at that time to the KLV experience. I grew up in a world in which a rigid pecking order prevailed and it was everyone for himself. In camp any feelings of sympathy or solidarity were systematically knocked out of me—except for my short friendship with Sagirashwili. (I was later told that shortly before the Red Army marched into Berlin, his father, in an act of political despair, shot his wife, his son, and his daughter.) In camp I had learned that in difficult times every man is his own best friend. This meant that in order to avoid being teased, despised, or beaten by the others you had to refrain at all costs from exposing any of your weak points. Therefore, I had conditioned myself—like Thomas Mann's Aschen-bach, the hero of *Death in Venice*—to live with "clenched fists," always on the defensive, never trusting anyone. On top of that I was forced to exercise strict self-control by my speech impediment, which might well have disappeared by itself after puberty, had it not been for the traumatic camp experiences. I could never relax and always had to have a synonym ready in case I got stuck on a particular word.

Consequently, although I felt a child's attachment to my mother, I also tried to assert myself against her in those first months after the war. I was closer to her than to my father and brother, but not so close that I would have written to her in Kassel during my time in Rauischholzhausen. Nor did I have much contact with my brother, who, after a brief stint in a prisoner-of-war camp near Bad Kreuznach, also found a job working for a dairy farmer in Rauischholzhausen. After my long oppression in the KLV, I probably was thinking only of myself and how I could get ahead. So when Mr. Kaiser sounded me out about whether I'd like to take over the farm, I accepted without hesitation. I even found his wish to adopt me and his suggestion that I call myself Jost Kaiser quite acceptable, since it seemed to me the most wonderful thing in the world to own a farmstead like his.[5]

As a good son I had been supplying my parents with flour, oatmeal, and rapeseed oil that I received in lieu of wages. But when they heard of Mr. Kaiser's adoption plans in the spring of 1946, they promptly intervened and brought me back to Kassel. There they rented a room for me in an elderly lady's apartment five houses down the street. They registered me, very much against my will, as a sixth-year student in secondary school, the *Realgymnasium* on Kölnische Strasse. And with that, my dream of making my own way in life came to an abrupt end and had to be replaced by a new dream. Only today can I see clearly how much my KLV experiences influenced me during this radical reorientation. Simply put, in the next few years I firmly rejected everything that had been so roughly imposed on us in the camp, while, on the other hand, all the things we had to give up in the Warthegau had an increasingly strong attraction for me.

I had come to detest any kind of drill. I hated sports so much that I asked to be excused from these activities in school. To my utter dismay, there was hardly a teacher in our school whose passion for learning could have instilled in us a belief in the deeper meaning of knowledge. Instead of engaging us in discussions about fundamental ideas and concepts or familiarizing us with important literary works, our teachers merely drummed formulas, grammatical constructions, and vocabulary into us. In addition, most of my classmates had spent the war years attending ordinary secondary schools in towns like Fritzlar, Korbach, Fulda, or Marburg, and I was so far behind them that I scarcely dared open my mouth in class, especially in English and Latin, of which I had only the most rudimentary knowledge. As for chemistry and physics, I knew nothing beyond how to use a Bunsen burner, and that you need a warm air current to get a glider flying. I didn't even know how to spell correctly, something any student my age certainly should know. I owe my promotion in October 1946 into the seventh-year class (*Obersekunda*) almost exclusively to the boy with whom I shared a desk and who allowed me to surreptitiously copy the important passages of many assignments and tests.

Socially, I also felt at a distinct disadvantage. In contrast to the Hindenburg Park secondary school in Berlin, where the majority of the students came from working-class or office workers' families, in Kassel I was thrown together with a group made up predominantly of the sons of doctors, lawyers, and senior government officials. I was far behind these middle-class sons not only in academic knowledge but also in manners and etiquette.

Because of my big-city and camp experiences, the only

place I did not trail these boys was in my sexual knowledge. Two of my sheltered classmates, at sixteen both still children, were constantly plagued by guilt feelings after they discovered masturbation; one even contemplated suicide. While they still had great inhibitions dealing with the girls from the Heinrich Schütz School, I was already going out dancing with a young hairdresser, and in spite of my stutter I was far less awkward with girls than they were.

I could thus be considered the sole "barbarian" in this class, which produced several well-known scientists, politicians, and lawyers. Yet despite the disparity in knowledge and social status, I had one thing in common with my classmates, namely, the yearning for "higher things" in the cultural sphere. Like most of those who were preparing for their final examination (*Abitur*) between 1947 and 1949, I counted myself among the "select few," the 4.5 percent of my generation who were proud to be *Gymnasiasten* and who would have considered it beneath them to listen to popular songs, to watch current movies, or to leaf through popular magazines.[6] For us the only thing that mattered in those years was Culture. Indeed, it probably meant more to me than to the other boys, who had grown up in refined homes and had been exposed from an early age to the finer things in life. I had an enormous desire to catch up.

In contrast to them, I was unfamiliar with classical music, serious literature (that is to say, works beyond *Winnetou* or *Rasputin*) as well as great art, and I was now intent on learning as much as I could, both theoretically and practically. During those years, I frequently went to the theater, listened to a great deal of classical music, and read innumerable novels and art books. I took up piano lessons, which I had stopped when I was twelve. Moreover, I registered at the Kassel School for Applied Arts for a class in drawing the nude taught by Mr. Kneisel, and I began to write my first poems in the style of Hermann Hesse and later Gottfried Benn. In 1949, at the instigation of a teacher who told me that people with speech impediments, like the famous Austrian, Ferdinand Raimund, often turned out to be top-notch actors, I made my stage debut in the Blue Room of the Kassel Municipal Hall as the protagonist in Goethe's *Epimenides' Awakening* (*Des Epimenides Erwachen*). In addition, I sang second bass with a large choral group that performed eight-part motets.

I was especially delighted with two fine arts summer programs I attended at the Edersee and in the Sauerland (in North Rhine–Westphalia) in 1947–48. Here we were not only urged to draw, sing, and act, but one of the teachers, Dr. Kurt Berger, also talked to us about the debased anti-intellectual nature of National Socialist poetry. In these classes I became increasingly aware of something I had, till then, felt only instinctively—the utter hypocrisy and superficiality of the propaganda we had repeated or sung in camp so automatically. Unfortunately, these three lectures—I still have a meticulously written copy of my notes—were to remain the only critical discussion of Nazi poetry I heard at the time. I now realized that it contained no worthwhile ideals and merely tried to exhort its followers to toughness, battle, victory, and death.

During my years at the Kassel school, I took an enthusiastic interest in the humanities, Weimar classicism, and Protestant values. My efforts were supported primarily by my music teacher, Mr. Römhild, who had been associated with the music publishing house of Bärenreiter and was steeped in the tradition of Heinrich Schütz, Leonhard Lechner, and Johann Sebastian Bach. So-called modern works—abstract painting and twelve-tone music—for the most part left me cold, for I was searching for an ideological guide to some kind of universal principle. At first my attitude was disoriented and defensive as the supporters of a detached, ambivalent modernism pushed the classical heritage in the arts—associated with values such as trust, altruism, tolerance, noble-mindedness, freedom of thought, and humanism—into the background. In the nonrepresentational paintings of American abstract expressionists or the serial music of Schönberg's successors I saw nothing that encouraged my hopes for something different, something better. And the more I saw of modernism, the emptier, the more meaningless it seemed to me. This aversion became even stronger in 1948–49, when I began to read periodicals like *Melos* and *Das Kunstwerk*, in which such art was promoted as "great modernist art against Everyman" (*Hohe Kunst gegen jedermann*)—an expression of elitism and a panacea for the false popularizing tendencies of the National Socialist cultural policies.[7] And so I retreated in disappointment to the great works of the past, where, it seemed to me, I could glimpse the dream of a better future.

I experienced similar disappointments in the social sphere. After my long years in the Hitler Youth camps, where the only principle I learned was "dog eat dog," I naively expected that in the wake of the promised "democratic reeducation," society would become more unified, moving away from the Nazi imperative to either demonstrate the toughness that defines the leader or fall meekly back into the second or third rank. Indeed, I had the vain hope that, inspired by noble ideals, new organizations might provide an opportunity to rebuild a common destiny, replacing the false god of national identity with a vision of the welfare of society as a whole.

Of course, little or nothing of the sort happened. And what little did happen between 1947 and 1949 went largely unnoticed by us students. Hardly anyone, whether in school, in our families, or elsewhere, discussed political, economic, or social problems with us. Most people, especially those who had profited from National Socialism, kept silent about such things. Consequently, what was most important to us Gymnasiasten in those years was not fascism or the policies of the occupying powers, but school and the arts. None of us read political commentaries in the newspapers. We turned on the radio only when there were symphonic or chamber music concerts; we didn't care a fig about the news. During midmorning breaks, I don't think we ever talked about the formation of the tripartite occupation zone in the West, the Marshall Plan, the ceremony in Frankfurt's St. Paul's Church to commemorate the 1848 revolution, the Hessian Constitution, the referendum on socialization of key industries, or the currency reform. Even the adoption of the West German constitution on 25 May 1949, and the first West German Bundestag elections on 19 August of that year, left us largely indifferent. Nor were we galvanized by the programs of the various parties, whether of the SPD (Social Democratic Party) and the KPD (German Communist Party) on the one hand or the CDU (Christian Democratic Union), FDP (Free Democratic Party), DP (German Party), and the BHE (*Bund der Heimatvertriebenen und Entrechteten*, League of People Expelled from Their Homeland and Deprived of Their Rights) on the other. We regarded all these alphabet soup organizations as insignificant, even contemptible, because they weren't idealistic and lacked culture. It seemed absurd to us to become involved with one of these parties. Politics still appeared to us paradoxically either as something decided only at higher levels where we had no influence anyway or as the result of a coming together of people of goodwill.

And therefore—whether out of ignorance or blind idealism—I saw no reason to grapple with the political problems of the day, or to join one of the young peoples' groups of the existing parties. The Federal Republic of Germany was established on 15 September 1949—shortly before we took our final examination—and I realized helplessly that, even though it was founded on the principle of antitotalitarianism, the new state did not take steps against Germany's fascist past with a constitutional commitment to the collective good. Rather, it rejected not only socialist ideology but also all ideological impulses inspired by the humanistic Weimar tradition and Christian altruism. The only "higher" demands we witnessed at the beginning of the fifties were those deluded Western calls for a crusade against the East, which were clearly a by-product of the cold war. On the other hand, we paid even less attention to statements made by the Marxist-oriented SPD, KPD, the Falken (Hawks) or the VVN (*Verein der Verfolgten des Naziregimes*, Association of the Victims of the Nazi Regime).

Meanwhile, we were constantly bombarded with news of West German economic triumphs. Among these were reports about the beneficial effects of the Marshall Plan, which got under way in 1947; the halt to the dismantling of German industry that followed the Petersberg Accord in November 1949; membership in the European Council in May 1950; and the successful founding in April 1951 of the Western European Coal and Steel Community. Our political ideals were considerably loftier but unspecific, and we got very little satisfaction from the programs of the various political parties and from reports that presented the economic miracle in a tone consciously devoid of ideology. We were especially put off by the pragmatic views of Ludwig Erhard (then CDU minister of economic affairs) on the problem of social coexistence. He declared that the Federal Republic of Germany was primarily an "economic entity" that could exist without an ideological foundation and whose primary task consisted in "setting up the fewest possible barriers to the individual's drive toward profit."[8]

Anyone who, because of his antifascist mentality, was searching for new cultural and philosophical ideals was bound to be dissatisfied with such pronouncements emphasizing individual greed. Yet in the early fifties, there were few statements other than those dealing with economic miracles—despite the fact that the principle of the social obligation and responsibility that comes with property was anchored in the constitution.

I therefore kept mostly to myself during the following years, immersing myself in the study of German language and literature at Marburg, which in those days was still an isolated university town. Most graduates in the German department became high school teachers. I pursued my studies even though, because of my speech impediment, I could see no practical future in the education field. I was full of undefined yearnings for a different, a better, society and for art sustained by lofty ideals. In those days I saw no opportunity to get involved in anything that "superseded individual interests." Self-assertion and individual talent was all that mattered if one wanted to get a high grade for a seminar. This applied even at the level of German literary studies, where the focus was ostensibly on the great writers, such as Goethe, Hölderlin, Stifter, and Rilke. I realized that I could succeed only through extensive written work, for I was not able to contribute to the oral discussions. Any collective endeavors were ridiculed—or else remained hidden from us. Neither I nor any of my fellow students knew that a political science curriculum had already been established in Marburg and that Wolfgang Abendroth had been teaching there since 1951.[9] Most of us in the German department merely thought of ourselves as students and nothing else. We qualified as doctoral candidates or candidates for the state examinations for teacher certification without setting any progressive political goals for ourselves.

This omission had some deplorable results. One might have thought that after their degrading experiences under fascism, whether in the army, the Hitler Youth, or the KLV camps, the West German people would opt for a goverment based on freedom, equality, and brotherhood or at least a sense of solidarity. But many of my generation, even those who were university students, and from whom one might expect some critical thinking, took their places in a social pyramid defined by the principle of individual striving for success. As always, it was primarily toughness of character that qualified one for the top positions.[10] Anyone who was halfway talented and had gone through some National Socialist training was able to assert himself yet again. The less hardened ones, those who hadn't gone through such training, who had deeper feelings or more social conscience, lost out once more. And so the KLV experience, like other forms of National Socialist education, continued to have its effect. Not only people of the older generation, but many in their twenties or thirties as well, tried to appear forceful if not downright authoritarian—or else they withdrew and, having been burned by fascism, retreated to the familiar position of *ohne mich* (leave me out).[11] Not until the second half of the fifties was there an ideological renewal, for example, in the campaigns against militarization and atomic warfare. But this belongs to a new page of German history, which has always been characterized by a complicated pattern of political repetition and progression, continuity and discontinuity.

EPILOGUE

A Journey into the Past

September 1991

▼

Again and again as I was writing the quasi-memoir sections of this book there were moments when memory failed me. Indeed, sometimes I had the feeling that things or events I had just described never really happened—that Kirchenpopowo and Gross-Ottingen had only been imagined places of horror, invented after the fact so that I could include myself among the victims of fascism. After all, some psychoanalysts claim that masochistically inclined people experience blissful relief by daydreaming themselves into little self-created hells. In writing autobiography, especially when no documents exist to limit the uninhibited flow of recollections, there is the distinct danger of enjoying one's martyrdom. I would like to think that my view of the past is free of such self-pity. Yet, on an unconscious level, I don't know whether that is so.

For that reason, once I had completed the first draft of this book, I decided to fly to Berlin from Madison, Wisconsin, where I have been working for the last thirty-nine years. From Berlin I planned to drive to the former Warthegau to try to find some of the buildings and villages where the events described in this book took place. The impetus for the trip was my discovery, after a long search in the university library in Madison, of "Popowo Kirch." on a 1912 map of the province of Poznań. So Kirchenpopowo actually existed! However, I could find neither Gross-Ottingen nor the neighboring villages of Neu Grabia and Standau on this or any more recent maps.

Hoping to unearth new information, I started my search for clues in Berlin. My old high school on the Blissestrasse in Wilmersdorf had survived the war quite well. It was no longer called Paul von Hindenburg School but was now the Friedrich Ebert School, and it looked considerably smaller than in 1940 when I, a timid ten-year-old, first walked in. But it was still the same beautiful, dignified building, constructed in the pre–World War I style I had found impressive even as a boy. In refurbishing the exterior, the municipal authorities had gone all-out to do it the honor it deserved. The same applied to the interior of the building. The walls had been newly painted, the floors polished to a shine, the bannisters on the stairs were artfully restored. Nevertheless, the atmosphere was singularly depressing. Crazies had had a field day with spray paint on the walls, stairwells, and doors, covering them with their Americanized but, as far as I was concerned, incomprehensible squiggles. Newspapers and magazines were piled up in the corners of the classrooms. The students, dressed in their casual fashions, sat around on the floor because that apparently was considered particularly "cool." The contradiction of freedom was prevalent here, as well as on the streets and in the stores of Berlin. The students meant to give an impression of nonchalant individuality, but in fact demonstrated their slavish conformity to the dictates of department store advertising and the designers who dominate fashion. Almost every one of them wore an unpaid advertisement on his or her T-shirt for some big firm or other, most of them American. One of the female students was wearing stone-washed jeans; on the right rear pocket was the word "pretty," and in the crotch area the word "woman" appeared. Not one of the boys even glanced at her jeans. I had the feeling I was in a semi-colonial satellite state, and that Germany had adopted the worst aspects of U.S. consumerism.

The old school benches had disappeared from the classrooms. In their stead, chairs had been arranged in an intentionally disorderly circle. The music room and the biology labs on the second floor no longer looked as immaculate as they once had. Although it was recess, the students' mood was subdued, almost listless. Most of them didn't even appear to notice the gray-haired fellow walking in their midst, searching in vain for the boy he once had been. In the office, I asked a friendly but uninterested secretary about the school's history. She said there was a school archive, but she didn't have the time just now to rummage around in it. Could I come back next week sometime? I left her my address and a short wish list. What I would like to have, I explained, were the names of all the teachers who taught at the school between 1940 and 1945, as well as a list of graduates for the year 1949. Once I had this information I hoped to find some of the boys who had been with me in various KLV camps during the war years but who had not left Berlin in 1945, as I had.

Outside in the Volkspark that used to be Hindenburg Park a few bums, surrounded by piles of empty beer bottles, were asleep on the benches. I went up Mecklenburgische Strasse, which had been my regular route to school. Almost no one walks on this street nowadays. Most people drive through it on their way elsewhere. The ugly firewalls of the undamaged houses were painted with obscenities and slogans: "New boys just arrived from the GDR," "Badly damaged," "We want power," and "Fuck off." As a result of a street-widening project, the beautiful Jugendstil subway entrance at Heidelberger Platz with its dark blue and turquoise majolica tiles had been replaced by unattractive new sidewalk entrances on either side. The S-

Bahn terminal at the Schmargendorfer Platz had fared even worse. It had been largely demolished, and the former ticket hall had been rebuilt and turned into a disco, its shoddiness accentuated by garish advertisements. Behind it, there used to be neatly kept and decorative community gardens (*Schrebergärten*), where—I suddenly remembered—before the war you could buy little bouquets of summer flowers for ten pfennig. Now a huge power plant with three smokestacks loomed over the area. The remains of our house at 4 Bingerstrasse had been torn down—probably in the fifties or sixties—and a functional boxlike building stood in its place.

Even before the Second World War, the neighborhood had not been particularly attractive, but today it looked utterly dilapidated. The process of change that I had already observed in my former school was evident all around. Consumer mentality, real estate speculation, and a jungle of advertisements had placed the stamp of shoddy commercialism on the area. Scarcely anyone spent his youth here anymore. Just as in Milwaukee or Chicago, people who lived in the better residential neighborhoods drove as fast as they could to central Berlin on two concrete city highways that crossed over the Mecklenburgische Strasse. The place seemed uninhabitable, suited only for passing through.

When I came back to my hotel near the zoo, I leafed through two thick Berlin phonebooks, looking for the names of former classmates. But I soon gave up, for there were dozens, if not hundreds, of entries under Bock, Giesecke, Horke, Michaelis, Reuter, and Wagner, and none of the first names sounded familiar. In the KLV camps we had never used each other's first names anyway, only our last. I was called "Hermand." And so the first stage of my search for clues was largely fruitless. But it had made me aware of how, in my former school and on the streets surrounding it, a vague liberalness, economic prosperity, tacky commercialism, and joyless egoism had replaced the Prussian sense of order, Protestant cleanliness, and fascist terror of my past.

The following morning I took the train to Poznań, Poland. There was even less to remind me of the 1940s there, as the old city had been almost completely destroyed toward the end of the war. That same afternoon two Polish friends, the Orlowskis, whom I had told of my project, drove me to Kirchenpopowo. On the map it was identified as Popowo Kościelna, "Place of the Church." Even though this little town was only fifteen miles (22 km) from Poznań, my friends had never heard of it and were curious to explore it. When we finally found the place after a lot of asking for directions, it turned out to be a tiny hamlet of perhaps twenty-five houses, with two somewhat larger buildings, a church and a school. The school must have been built around 1910 by the Prussian authorities in the rural building style of the day. My friends were disappointed when I told them that I didn't remember it at all. Not until I saw the back entrance did I recall that two of the teachers had lived there. Since it was late afternoon, the building was locked. Behind it—where as ten-year-olds we had planted small flower beds under Dr. Fette's supervision and where we had played Völkerball on a carefully leveled field—there was now an ugly soccer field lined with old car tires. Beyond it, as in 1940, were farmlands and meadows. The school and the other buildings in the village seemed even poorer than I remembered. The grocery store and the post office had vanished. The only new building was a large black-stained wooden church, which towered over the entire village. On its front facade golden letters proclaimed "1629–1955," but the church, only a hundred yards from the school, had not been there in the forties. It had obviously been rebuilt later according to old plans.

As we were driving out of the village—my friends were silent but surely full of unspoken questions about their past and mine—I saw a small pond and next to it a white-painted stone road marker. These lone details were suddenly sharp in my mind: I have a photograph, taken by my mother with our old Voigtländer camera, in which I am sitting on the same stone marker in front of the same pond dressed in my winter uniform.

Several of the large swampy meadows west of Popowo Kościelna, like the beautiful wetlands around Madison, had been sacrificed to progress, and with them the innumerable lapwings that used to nest there. I was happy, after a little searching, to spot two of these birds so closely connected in my memory with Dr. Fette, as were the little flower beds behind the old schoolhouse. On the return trip we drove past Lake Lechlin and through Skoki, which was called Schocken in 1940. When I saw the railway station there, I remembered how we had arrived in Kirchenpopowo. Not on buses. Instead, a small train with a constantly ringing bell took us from Posen to Schocken, and from there several hay wagons had carried us the rest of the way.

All in all, I gleaned very little from this short detour, from which I had hoped to unleash a stream of inspiration. Almost nothing triggered memories. But the smallness and remoteness of the place impressed itself upon me; no wonder it had seemed like "the asshole of the world" to us boys coming from a metropolis like Berlin.

The trip to Gross-Ottingen was quite different. I hired a taxi in Poznań—feeling embarrassed by this display of Western prosperity. The driver understood a little German. I said I was looking for a village that was called Gross-Ottingen in the years between 1939 and 1945. I still remembered its approximate location—somewhere between Inowrocław (formerly Hohensałza) and Aleksandrów Kujawski (Alexandrowo). I told him the name probably began with an "O." The neighboring village, I said, was called Neu Grabia during the German occupation. The driver seemed glad to get a lucrative fare, and we started off the next morning. Until we reached Gniezno, the road from Poznań was excellent. It connected the Poznań and Gniezno cathedrals and, my driver informed me, was consequently "subsidized" by the Vatican. On both sides of the road there were new minibars, hot dog stands, Pepsi Cola advertisements, and posters identifying industrial or small-scale joint ventures. American rock music droned from the taxi's radio, and I felt as though I were on the highway connecting Madison and Chicago. When the radio suddenly switched to serious music—Polish art songs to be exact—the driver immediately shoved a tape with more American rock music into his cassette player and pushed the "play" button. The diesel trucks in front of us were pouring forth thick black clouds of soot, forcing us to keep our windows closed. Along the sides of the road lay the carcasses of cats and rabbits flattened by car tires. It wasn't much different from driving through the state of Hesse in Germany or Wisconsin in the United States.

The cathedral of Gniezno, which stands on a hill near the Warthe River, is a carefully tended showpiece. Workmen were paving the churchyard with handsome flagstones. And inside, too, the cathedral had been faultlessly restored. From Inowrocław we drove on to Gniewkowo. There, I asked the driver to turn off to the right. As soon as we left the main road, the countryside became much more peaceful. When we reached the next village, Murzynno, time seemed to have stood still for half a century. There were hardly any people, to say nothing of cars. We found a farmer, and when the taxi driver asked him how to get to Grabia, he pointed sullenly to the east. The countryside became even more isolated. After crisscrossing a landscape of irregular beet fields, woodlands, and barren places, we suddenly saw a sign pointing to the village of "Opoczki." The name made me curious, even though it awoke no memories. Here too we saw no people anywhere. But then, at the end of the village, we came upon an old man, surely in his eighties. The taxi driver asked him where Grabia was, explaining that he was trying to find it for a foreign passenger. The man turned to me and said in German, "This used to be Klein-Ottingen. If you continue on this road, you'll first get to Gross-Ottingen and then to Grabia."

We followed that road—the same one I had to march on, back and forth, over and over, as a Hitler Youth in 1943–44—until we arrived in Opoczki. This was it: a tiny village with low houses and no conspicuous new buildings. Only the electric power lines and an asphalt-paved street were new. At the end of the village—finally!—I spotted the red schoolhouse I had been looking for. It looked much as I remembered it. The brick exterior had held up well, but all the rest seemed pretty neglected. The water pump was gone. The disgusting outhouse, on the other hand, was still there. Apparently, the aging barn was no longer in use and was moldering away. In the back half of the schoolyard, which we always had to rake and sweep clean, were piles of ash and garbage. The front part had been converted into a basketball court.

After I had taken several photographs, two dozen children suddenly stormed noisily out into the schoolyard. I took this opportunity to go inside. In the hall I met the teacher. She spoke to me in Polish, and I answered her in English, too embarrassed to speak German. Baffled, she just left me standing there and went out into the yard.

Where once there had been beds and lockers there were now, just as in the Friedrich Ebert School in Berlin, a few chairs placed in a circle. The dining hall upstairs had been divided into two rooms. The classrooms and the stairwell seemed terribly narrow, and it was hard to imagine that once this building had housed fifty boys, a camp

The schoolhouse in Opoczki (September 1991). Photograph by Jost Hermand.

squad leader, a housekeeper, and a nurse. The Polish schoolchildren scarcely took notice of me, but all of them gaped in admiration at the taxi, which must have been one of the first to have come to the village. Here too, external appearance seemed to be ruled by the same contradictions as in West Berlin: Everything seemed more slovenly compared to the old days, but at the same time more relaxed, free of the constraints of totalitarianism, indeed, of any purposeful desire for order.

The taxi driver, with whom I had been having a lively conversation up to then, was silent as we drove on. He probably couldn't understand why I had come all the way from the United States to see this forsaken little village with its shabby schoolhouse. He had grown up in Poznań after 1950 and therefore had no memories of the time when Poles and Germans faced each other in this region as deadly enemies. He probably thought it extremely odd that I, a Westerner who could afford to buy anything I desired, should want to see an unattractive Polish village like Opoczki. And I, too, suddenly felt as though I had come to the end of the earth: maps were no longer reliable, hardly anything had changed in decades, there were no cars, and an eerie quiet reigned. For older people like me who had lived here before 1945, the bloody past was still lurking behind the facade of sleepy provinciality.

Neu Grabia, which is called Grabie today, seemed a lot less familiar to me. Unlike Opoczki, it had a small church. Next door to it, surrounded by a wall, was the building in which the Polish nurse had saved my life (for which I had never had a chance to thank her). I didn't understand what the sign at the entrance said, and the taxi driver couldn't explain it to me in German. After a few laborious attempts he finally said, "Little children, not parents." Evidently the building was now a Catholic orphanage, no longer, as it we had been told, a prison for young Polish "criminals." It was located in a quiet setting, behind a garden gone wild and shaded by old trees. In this village, too, there seemed to be very few people.

My thoughts began to wander. I still couldn't believe that I, who had spent most of my life in West Germany and the United States, had marched as a Pimpf through this part of Poland five decades ago, singing "Forward, forward! the bright trumpets blare. Forward, forward! Youth knows no dangers." Between 1940 and 1945 this part of the Nazi Warthegau had been even more remote and backward. After all, today Opoczki has running water and electricity, and if you have the necessary hard currency you can even be driven there in a relatively comfortable taxi. These thoughts moved me deeply, and I was no longer able to talk with the driver about trivial things that didn't strain his meager German vocabulary. And yet I was thinking about him, too. I wondered what kind of person he thought I was: a curious tourist, a former Nazi, an arrogant Westerner, or merely a paying passenger?

I had asked myself some of these same questions in Poznań when I was with my Polish friends, although I didn't dare to voice them. Did my friends see me as a pushy self-centered fellow who could afford to run after his vanished youth, or did they see me as a German seriously trying to come to grips with his past? While pondering these questions, I remembered how embarrassed I was in 1972 when I met the Polish art historian Jan Bialistocki in the United States. We decided to speak English rather than German, although the latter would have been easier for both of us. After the first awkward moments, I asked him where he was when the war ended. "In Mauthausen concentration camp," he said. "To keep them from killing me, I drew Hans Thoma–style greeting and birthday cards for SS officers." When he asked me the same question, I answered, "In Krotoschin, just as some Poles were beginning to kill or beat up Germans who hadn't managed to make the last train going west." Two years later at an art historians' convention in Hamburg, we thought it best to limit our discussion to art.

Three days after my visit to Opoczki, I left Poland and returned to Berlin. I immediately called my old school to find out what I could about my former teachers and classmates. When I refused to be put off, the secretary, who was obviously not familiar with the archives, suggested I call the alumni association, which, she thought, must still have some of the documents relating to that time. But the alumni association was no more accommodating than the school. The alumni president put me off for weeks, and then he just didn't call back. Could be that he saw in me someone who wanted to foul their nest. But it's also possible that all the documents relating to those days had been destroyed. In any case, my second attempt to get more details about the Paul von Hindenburg High School during the Second World War fizzled.[1] Research at the Koblenz Federal Archives was just as fruitless. Even though they had many KLV files, there was nothing about the particular camps in the former Warthegau that interested me.[2] The Bochum KLV Documentation Study Group, to whom the Federal Archives had referred me, also had nothing worth mentioning on the subject.[3]

Thus, even though I would have liked to broaden the subjective process of recollection, it remained for the most part a one-man stalking project. Again and again my inquiries came up against a wall of silence, barely concealed indifference, scornful shrugs, or other defense mechanisms. Scarcely anybody wanted to be reminded of the "Brown Shirt" years before 1945. Even the subject of the "Children's Evacuation Program" was taboo, although—given the ages of the participating children and young people—no direct questions of guilt could have been raised. After all, this was not an investigation having to do with membership in Party organizations like the Stormtroopers and the SS or complicity in the extermination of Jews, or participation the campaigns against partisans in Poland and Russia which resulted in the murder of millions of people. The only Germans who were still trying to keep alive the memories of the KLV action were a few unregenerate Nazis. When I spoke with other students of my generation who had been *verschleppt* (dragged off) to these Hitler Youth camps, most of them told me they considered this episode in their lives over and done with.

And so I decided to give in to the inevitable, limiting myself to my own recollections, especially since the broad spectrum of my memories seemed sufficient to shed light on the KLV phenomenon from several angles. But one day I suddenly remembered the first name of one of the boys with whom I had been in camp both in Kirchenpopowo and in Gross-Ottingen. It turned out he still lived in Berlin. I telephoned him. After his initial surprise, he remembered me quite well and readily answered all the questions I had prepared in advance about our joint KLV experiences. After I had filled up several pages with his answers, the stream of recollections began to diminish. In our second phone conversation, he didn't have much to add. I asked him whether he remembered any of the other boys from those days or whether he had kept in touch with them. Indeed, he had, but unfortunately there weren't many. Few of the former students from Paul von Hindenburg High School had stayed in Berlin after the war. Of these, only three had graduated in 1948–49 from the new Friedrich Ebert School, which took the place of the Hindenburg, Treitschke, and Fichte High Schools. But still, there were three, and when I telephoned one of them, he remembered two other names.

So finally I was able to contact six of my former Berlin classmates. They readily answered my increasingly pointed questions, and after two days I had almost twenty pages of letter-size paper tightly covered with handwritten notes: new facts, stories, names, experiences, dates. One of them even sent me a publication by an association of former students, teachers, and friends of the Friedrich Ebert School in Berlin-Wilmersdorf, which contained a complete list of all graduates after 1945, as well as the names of the teachers who had been at the school right after the war. At last I had the lists that the school secretary and the chairman of the alumni association had not been able to get for me. Another of my former classmates was even able to come up with the name and address of one of the three camp squad leaders. This man, who was born in 1926, lived in Berlin and provided me with additional information.

At first I was quite at a loss to know how I was going to accommodate this new information in my already finished book. Much of it coincided with or complemented my recollections. But some of the material contradicted my memories on important points. When I tried to insert these new facts and conclusions in my cleanly typed manuscript, I felt instinctively that they would undermine my intent to work from *my own* recollections. But what else could I do with them? Then I suddenly came up with the idea of weaving these new facts and stories into an epilogue. In this way I would approach the obviously problematic process of remembering in a new way, by also presenting the memories of others. Thus, instead of merely appending new facts to the book as a whole or bitter experiences to various anecdotes, the new material would give my report a second, wider dimension. At the same time, it would show that in spite of our shared experiences, each one of us who had been in the KLV camps lived his own story and preserved it in a more or less truthful, stylized, or falsified form.

But before I go too far into theorizing on this point—to which some space will be devoted later—I would like to take a look at the collective and individual significance of the new material. Only three of the people I spoke to had been in Kirchenpopowo. Two of them had only vague recollections of the camp and couldn't even remember the teachers there. The only fresh information they contributed was to point out that Kirchenpopowo did not have electricity. To remedy the problem, they said, the members of the Luftwaffe who were quartered in the right wing of the schoolhouse had set up a big generator in the cellar; we shared its benefits. I didn't have the foggiest recollection of any of this, but my informant, an engineer, remembered it in great detail.

I also learned that in the summer of 1942, while I was in San Remo, part of my class was sent to a KLV camp in Bad Joachimsthal in the Erz Mountains. None of the men I interviewed had any lasting impressions of this camp. On the other hand, because of the hardships they endured in Gross-Ottingen, they clearly remembered their time there and expressed the most negative feelings about the squad leaders who were in charge of us. And yet even on this point there were definite differences of opinion. Some said that the "exaggerated Hitler Youth drill" that predominated "was entirely routine" during "those times," just as everything "active" and "athletic" was. Others said that two of the camp squad leaders who had imposed "extreme punishments" would be labeled "sadists" today. Sometimes, they recalled, the leaders didn't hesitate to beat boys with their "billy clubs," or lock them into the latrine "for hours at a time." The second one in particular had "always allowed things to go to extremes." My six sources and I could remember the name of the first camp squad leader, but not of the other two. I was told that some boys had called the second one "Schielewip" behind his back because he was cross-eyed. Indeed, one of my informants even claimed that he had vigorously complained to the district authorities in Standau about our harsh treatment in the camp. As a result, an on-site inspection commission had described the lock-ups in the latrine as "bolshevist torture methods" and had insisted on the immediate abolition of such practices.

In contrast to the reports of my former classmates in which the camp squad leader always functioned as the highest authority, a former camp squad leader told me he was only the intermediary between the all-powerful camp director and us boys. Even though I knew that he had been an *Oberscharführer* (equivalent to technical sergeant in the U.S. Army) with the Hitler Youth Patrol and had taken a training course as camp squad leader in a special camp in Neustadt on the Dosse, he made himself out to be just "one of the boys" who had taken our side on many occasions. In the wintertime, he said, he had several times climbed with us across the barn roof into one of the supply rooms to steal the coal that Miss Sommer, the housekeeper, distributed so stingily. He said he also could still remember how he had joined a group that included me on a trip to the cemetery in a neighboring village. There, he said, we had dug up the zinc coffin of an eighteenth-century Polish aristocrat in order to procure a well-preserved human skull for class. He had found it a hell of a job to remove the mummified skin from the cranium and cheekbones. First he had soaked the head in one of the wooden tubs in the cellar in which we all took our weekly hot baths, and then he had hung it up to dry in the chimney shaft. But all his efforts were in vain, and so he threw away the half-boiled, half-charred head. What he remembered best, he assured me, was a horse named Schutger, which he rode twice a week to the home of a noblewoman who owned a nearby estate and who gave him lessons in Latin and English.

My former classmates and this camp squad leader had considerably less to say about the teachers in Gross-Ottin-gen. There was only one whom they all remembered well: Mr. Quastenberg, nicknamed "Qualle" (Jellyfish). He was our camp director and English teacher. Oddly enough, I don't remember him at all. Apparently, he lived in the schoolhouse with us, and in spite of his sixty years always tried to look like a snappy officer. As a deeply committed Nazi, he constantly raised his arm in the Hitler salute and wore a fancy black uniform reminiscent of the SS. Most of my sources also remembered our math teacher, Dr. Her-mann Meyer, who signed all our classwork papers "Dr. My" and whom we therefore called "Dr. Mü."[4] As a "non-Nazi," he had kept clear of administrative matters, always insisting, "I have no say in this." The only thing that stuck in their minds about our drawing teacher, Mr. Stuller, was that he had had a "relationship" with the assistant house-keeper, Angelica. Their recollections of the music teacher, Mr. Lubczik, whose real name was in fact Romuald Lub-czyk, were just as limited. The only reason he made any impression on them at all was because of his strictness and the drumstick he used to hit us. Nor could my informants tell me very much about Nurse Charlotte, but a few remembered one thing clearly: a soldier had spent several nights in her room, and she had introduced him to us as her fiancé.

It was interesting to hear how my camp mates described the other boys, but there was nothing new in what they had to say. However, I found a few facts revealing. First, the Gross-Ottingen camp had housed not only boys who were born in 1930, but also those born in 1929. So we were taught in two separate classes, and the older boys mercilessly tyrannized the younger children, of whom I was one. Second, we didn't all go to the SS ski camp on the Hohe Eule in Silesia; some boys were sent to an army medical training course and others to a Luftwaffe premilitary training camp in Schneidemühl. There, in July 1944, they had to take basic examinations in glider flying as part of their training.

In general, most of my sources knew more about the years 1944–45, when we were already fourteen to sixteen years old, than about the time they had spent in the camps during the early phase of the war. Specifically, they provided me with new material about the Sulmierschütz camp. For one thing, it seems to have been much larger than I thought. Not only was it an extension of the Gross-Ottingen camp, but it also took in boys born in 1928 who had formerly been housed by the KLV administration in Leslau. Thus Director Krohn and Dr. Hilpert, our teachers, hadn't come straight from Berlin to Sulmierschütz, but had already participated in the Leslau camp. At Sulmierschütz, we were saddled with another math teacher and a Latin teacher named Guse, whom we called "Asinus." Some of my classmates remembered everyday things like food and washing much more vividly than I did.

I was surprised to learn that all these boys had gone on to still another camp the second week of February 1945. This camp was in Lanz near Lenzen, not far from Wittenberge on the Elbe. By chance, I had been saved from this because during that same week I was staying with my mother in a different apartment and had not gotten in touch with my school at Hindenburg Park. My classmates told me that our teachers from Sulmierschütz—Krohn,

Hitler Youth and Volkssturm soldier with antitank rocket launchers await-
ing an attack by Soviet tanks (April 1945). From H. W. Koch, Hitler
Youth: The Duped Generation *(New York: Ballantine Books, 1972).*

Hilpert, Guse, and Lubczyk—were also sent to Lanz. All
the boys and teachers were put up in a youth hostel where
the living conditions were "horrendous." In March, some
of my former classmates were ordered to join the *Panzer-
grenadierdivision Grossdeutschland* (Greater Germany Armored
Infantry Division) as the "last reserves" and to take part in
the defense of Berlin.[5] Many, among them Giesecke, Reich,
and Kropp, were killed in these final battles.[6] Those who
survived made their perilous way back to Berlin.

Some of the things I discovered about the final weeks of
the war touched me deeply. My friend Sagiraschwili,
whose first name was Schota, had not died at his father's
hands as I had believed for forty-five years. He had
escaped with his family to northern Italy and then to
Switzerland. There, having been a former Georgian general, author, and liaison to the Wlassow Army, his father was
granted political asylum. He was never found guilty of any
real crimes, and indeed published an "Open Letter to Stalin" in a Swiss newspaper in the summer or fall of 1945
to remove any suspicion that he had been a "fascist." All

along I had presumed my friend dead, and on hearing the true story, I felt enormous relief. One of my classmates confirmed that a family massacre in which nobody survived actually had taken place in our neighborhood, but it involved a family named Asche, not the Sagiraschwilis. The head of the Asche family, a high-ranking Nazi, decided in April 1945 to kill his entire family in Berlin, including his son, who had been with us in Gross-Ottingen.

The rest of the information I collected was less compelling. For instance, I was able to verify from the list of former teachers at my school that the occupation powers had fired Dr. Krohn from his position as school director in the fall of 1945, but that he had continued teaching for two more years, indicating that he had probably been classified merely as a *Mitläufer* (follower). Mr. Quastenberg, who had allegedly been a ruthless Nazi and had forced Jews to leave air raid shelters during the war, had to quit his school job after 1945. There were no traces of the other teachers, or of many of my classmates. I recognized only four names on the graduating lists for the years 1948–49. The others must have either escaped to the West, died or been killed during the war, or failed the school requirements of the postwar period.

And that closes this Camp Odyssey, which we began so naively. The journey caused us a lot of suffering, and ended—temporarily—during the utter chaos of the last months of the war. I emphasize "temporarily," because, whether we know it or not, all those who were caught up in the KLV are still marked by our experiences. Each of us has worked out his own story to suit himself. The stories may have many similarities, but they differ not only in the range of emotions they released in us, but in facts we recall. Had we who were in the camps shared the same feelings, had we been inspired by the same ideals, we would all have just *one* story to tell, one that varies only in detail. But because of the "dog eat dog" atmosphere of the camps, we were constantly on the defensive. Each of our stories is therefore overshadowed by the fear of others' brutality. In contrast to some of the old Nazis among the former camp squad leaders and KLV supervisors, the boys I knew—who are now old men—never looked back on their camp years with nostalgia. Indeed, however much they try to conceal it, admitting the trauma only in the presence of those who have gone through the same ordeal, many still suffer from the experiences of those years. Nevertheless, during conversations with KLV participants, I discovered a significant difference in their outlook: The more robust of them generally had a better recollection of what had taken place, that is, of factual matters, whereas the weaker ones did not remember the facts so much as the emotions and fears connected with them.

Therefore, one cannot say that the experiences of the Kinderlandverschickung are over and done with. Those caught up in the tentacles of this giant operation who adopt this view are only fooling themselves. If you look more closely, you'll see that what they endured as children affects them in countless ways today—in their thoughts, actions, emotions—whether in obsessive repetitive behavior or in conscious reactions against those old experiences. After all, during their most vulnerable years, in addition to coping with the turmoils of adolescent desire, envy, hate, guilt, and shame, they were subjected to the most extreme cruelty and humiliation. Such youthful injuries often have much more profound effects than wounds suffered in adulthood. It is true that many people tend to distance themselves from traumatic experiences with an I-don't-want-to-know-anything-about-it attitude. But over time, because of the repression of these memories, this can turn into I-can't-possibly-know-anything-about-it attitude.[7] Indeed, some KLV participants are oblivious to how their emotional frigidity, their selective interest in the things around them—their enormous self-centeredness—and their arrogance toward people they perceive as less intelligent, as weak, or dependent on them, all reflect the desire to subordinate others that was drilled into them in their youth. Thus, in spite of all efforts to distance oneself from these early traumas, the damage is in many cases easily seen—especially if you know the odd ways in which repressed elements tend to resurface.

It was therefore my aim in this book, in addition to presenting an abundance of empirical material relating to the KLV experience, to highlight some of the psychological mechanisms that operated in the camps, like the constant drive to assert oneself in the hierarchy. At the same time, I also wanted to indicate several possible responses to show what we went through. One response is critical reflection, the exposure and deconstruction of National Socialist myths like "comradeship," "honor," "courage," "sense of community," and "team spirit." But this kind of critique is not enough in itself. It must be accompanied by the "emotional work" described by Margarete Mitscherlich in her 1987 book *Errinerungsarbeit: Zur Psychoanalyse der Unfähigkeit zu trauern* (The work of remembering: On the psychoanalysis of the inability to mourn). Mitscherlich explores the function of memory as well as the consequence of not remembering. She feels that traumatic situations, with all their attendant feelings—hate, desire, cruelty, fear of death—have to be relived again and again. Only then, she writes, can one begin to counteract the devastation of what one has suffered. Unless this work is done, the increasingly entrenched traumas will lead to a "compulsive [and] neurotic repetition of the same [mistakes]" and thereby to a progressive "immobilization" of social conditions. She blames developments in today's Germany on the "sadomasochistic upbringing and character formation" during the Hitler era, the "obsequious identification with the powerful" and the "contempt for the weak" that have endured as a result of the "obscuration and misinformation among great sections of our society." She calls for a "process of learning how to let go" as a prerequisite to new ways of thinking.[8]

Thus, in addition to the task of critical reflection, my generation, so deeply affected by our youthful wartime experience, still face the psychological work of remembering our past in order to finally free ourselves for the future. If we do not rise to the challenge, we will not only be repeating what was drilled into us; even worse, we will be passing our unexamined attitudes on to others. And in this way, fascism will have achieved its goal after all, continuing to affect successive generations of Germans. We must guard against this by searching for a new social identity that will no longer rest on the principle of "might makes right."

NOTES

▼

INTRODUCTION
The Difficulties of Reappraising a Traumatic Experience

1. See, e.g., Horst Überhorst, ed., *Elite für die Diktatur: Die nationalpolitischen Erziehungsanstalten, 1933–1945* (An elite for the dictatorship: Nazi political educational institutions, 1933–1945) (Düsseldorf, 1969).

2. Among the exceptions are Ottwilm Ottweiler, *Die Volksschule im Nationalsozialismus* (Public schools in National Socialism) (Weinheim-Basel, 1979); Harald Focke and Uwe Reimer, "Schule," in *Alltag unterm Hakenkreuz* (Everyday life under the Swastika) (Reinbek, 1979); U. Popplow, "Schulalltag im Dritten Reich: Fallstudie über ein Göttinger Gymnasium" (School routine in the Third Reich: Case study of a Göttingen high school), in *Aus Politik und Zeitgeschichte* (Politics and contemporary history), supplement to *Das Parlament*, 3 May 1980, 33–69; Geert Platner, ed., *Schule im Dritten Reich—Erziehung zum Tod? Eine Dokumentation* (School in the Third Reich—education for death? Documents) (Munich, 1983). Cf. also Kurt-Ingo Flessau, *Schule und Diktatur: Lehrpläne und Schulbücher des Nationalsozialismus* (Schools and dictatorship: Lesson plans and schoolbooks of National Socialism) (Munich, 1977); and Willi Feiten, *Der nationalsozialistische Lehrerbund: Entwicklung und Organisation* (The National Socialist League of Teachers: Its development and organization) (Weinheim, 1981).

3. For additional information about the Kinderlandverschickung between 1933 and 1940, see, e.g., Peter Bucher, ed., *Wochenschauen und Dokumentarfilme 1895–1950 im Bundesarchiv* (Weekly newsreels and film documentaries in the German Federal Archive, 1895–1950) (Koblenz, 1984), 320ff.

4. The figure 2.8 million is cited by Dabel. See Gerhard Dabel,

KLV: Die erweiterte Kinderlandverschickung (Freiburg, 1981), 7. Würschinger in fact speaks of 3 million, and Larass of 5 million children who participated. Cf. Gottfried Griesmayr and Otto Würschinger, *Idee und Gestalt der Hitlerjugend* (The idea and form of the Hitler Youth) (Leonie, 1979), 263; and Claus Larass, *Der Zug der Kinder: KLV, die Evakuierung 5 Millionen deutscher Kinder im 2. Weltkrieg* (The procession of children: KLV, the evacuation of five million German children in the Second World War) (Munich, 1983). More skeptical authors question this figure and speak of only 800,000 KLV participants. Cf. Hans-Christian Brandenburg, *Die Geschichte der HJ: Wege und Irrwege einer Generation* (The story of the Hitler Youth: A generation led astray) (Cologne, 1968), 231; Arno Klönne, *Jugend im Dritten Reich: Die Hitler-Jugend und ihre Gegner* (Young people in the Third Reich: The Hitler Youth and its opponents) (Munich, 1980), 39; and Hilde Kammer and Elisabet Bartsch, *Jugendlexikon National-sozialismus: Begriffe aus der Zeit der Gewaltherrschaft, 1933–1945* (Young people's lexicon of National Socialism: Terms from the time of despotic rule, 1933–1945) (Reinbek, 1990), 106.

5. Politicians and other prominent figures (e.g., Helmut Kohl and Mildred Scheel) gave evasive answers when questioned by Dabel. See Dabel, *KLV*, 297.

6. Among the few exceptions in this field are a book for young readers by Frank Baer, *Die Magermilchbande* (The Skim Milk Gang) (1979), which deals with the adventurous return to Berlin from a KLV camp, and the KLV episode in Andreas Oko-penko's novel *Kindernazi* (Child Nazis) (1984), 28ff.

7. See, e.g., Michael Schneider, "Väter und Söhne, posthum.: Das beschädigte Verhältnis zwischen den Generationen" (Fathers and sons, posthum.: The damaged relationship between the generations), in *Den Kopf verkehrt aufgesetzt oder Die melancholische Linke* (Having your head on backwards, or The melancholy Left), ed. Michael Schneider (Darmstadt-Neuwied, 1982), 90–102; and Reinhold Grimm, "Elternspuren, Kindheitsmuster: Lebensdarstellung in der jüngsten deutschsprachigen Prosa" (Parental traces, childhood models: Descriptions of life in recent German literature), in *Vom Anderen und vom Selbst: Beiträge zu Fragen der Biographie und Autobiographie* (About the other and the

self: Contributions to the problems of biography and autobiography), ed. Reinhold Grimm and Jost Hermand (Königstein, 1982), 167–82.

8. Griesmayr and Würschinger, *Idee und Gestalt*, 7, 259.

9. Ibid., 7.

10. Jutta Rüdiger, ed., *Die Hitler-Jugend und ihr Selbstverständnis im Spiegel ihrer Aufgabengebiete* (Hitler Youth as it saw itself reflected in its assignments) (Lindhorst, 1983), 328.

11. Ibid., 297ff. Many of Rüdiger's arguments sound as though they had been written before 1945. For contemporary KLV propaganda, see Ingeborg Lohse, "In sicherer Hut: Jungens von der Waterkant im Hochgebirg zu Gast" (In safe keeping: Boys from the coast as guests in the mountains), *Neues Volk* 9 (August 1941): 4: "Protected from bombs dropped by English planes, [the KLV participants] are to have a carefree time here which will become a great and unforgettable experience for most of them."

12. According to Alfred Ehrentreich, *50 Jahre erlebte Schulreform* (Fifty years of school reform) (Frankfurt am Main, 1985), 148, Gerhard Dabel was a "former Hitler Youth leader." Between 1941 and 1942 Dabel had six books published by Verlag Junge Generation: *Das Gebot der Stunde: Verse für die Front* (The commandment of the hour: Verses for the front); *Grossstadtjungen: Der Weg einer jungen Mannschaft in die Zeit* (Big-city boys: The path of a youthful team into this period); *Kameraden der 100 Zelte* (Comrades in a hundred tents); *Mit Krad und Karabiner: Fahrt und Kampf einer Kradschützenschwadron* (With motorcycle and rifle: The journey and battle of a squadron of motorcycle riflemen); *Die Piraten von Moen* (The pirates of Moen); and *Der Rächer der Eifel* (The avenger of the Eifel). They were intended as reading material for squad leaders and Hitler Youth members of the Jungvolk. For Dabel's role in the KLV leadership, see also Rüdiger's *Die Hitler-Jugend*, 291.

13. See Jost Hermand, *Old Dreams of a New Reich: Volkish Utopias and National Socialism* (Bloomington, 1992), 243. Published in Germany under the title *Der alte Traum vom neuen Reich: Völkische Utopien und Nationalsozialismus* (Frankfurt am Main, 1988).

14. Dabel, *KLV, 7*.

15. Ibid., 42.

16. Dabel generally quotes positive reactions of KLV partici-pants in his document appendix: "A superb accomplishment," "an eventful and marvelous time," "many positive memories," "is among my most beautiful memories," "unforgettable," "a won-derful time," and so forth (310ff.). The collection of documents the book is based on is today a part of the Bundesarchiv in Koblenz (Call no.: ZGs 140).

17. See Larass, *Der Zug der Kinder*, 14. The following passage is an example of how Larass attempts to cover up his overall posi-tive attitude toward the KLV program: "The National So-cialist influence was surely a desired side-effect, as illustrated by numer-ous utterances of Hitler's. One cannot really credit him with the evacuations—such a humanitarian program cannot be credited to a man like Adolf Hitler, who out of criminal ambition embroiled a whole continent in war. At most, interpreting it very generously, one could say that he was not guilty of having committed a crime in this area. All of the 12,000 camps were directed by teachers who had started the journey with the students from the same hometown. If at all, then any positive end result of the program is due to the professional ethics of the teachers involved and the selfless work of their assistants. The camp squad leaders were Hitler Youth representatives. But hardly any of them were older than sixteen, seventeen, or eighteen; most were considerably younger and thereby an additional person in need of the teachers' care. There was to be no military drill in the camps" (15).

18. Ibid., 163, 164, 261, 262, 265, 267.

19. Ibid., 55.

20. See Hans-Jochen Gamm, *Führung und Verführung: Päda-gogik des Nationalsozialismus* (Leadership and seduction: National Socialist education) (Munich, 1964), 22ff., 48ff.

21. Cf. Henry Picker, *Hitlers Tischgespräche im Führer-haupt-quartier* (Hitler's conversations at table in the Führer's headquar-ters) (Munich, n.d.), 97, 119ff., 186f., 313ff., 366f.

22. See Nancy Vedder-Shults, "Motherhood for the Father-land: The Portrayal of Women in Nazi Propaganda" (Ph.D. diss., University of Wisconsin, Madison, 1982).

23. Gamm, *Führung und Verführung*, 26, 28.

24. Adolf Hitler, *Mein Kampf* (Munich, 1925), 451.

25. Cited in Gamm, *Führung und Verführung*, 60.

26. Cited in Walther Hofer, *Der Nationalsozialismus in Dokumenten* (National Socialism in documents) (Frankfurt am Main, 1957), 88.

27. Reprinted in *Ursachen und Folgen* (Causes and consequences) (Berlin, n.d.), 11:138f.

28. Cited in Gamm, *Führung und Verführung*, 50, and in Rolf Schörker, ed., *Das Dritte Reich* (Stuttgart, 1982), 15.

29. On 29 April 1937, speaking to 800 Nazi Party district leaders gathered at Ordensburg Sonthofen, Hitler said: "Only one man can command; one commands and the others must obey. That may of course be very difficult. But the intellect [of the leader of the state] also has a right and thus a duty: the right to take on dictatorial power, and the duty to force others to obey." Quoted in Norbert Frei, *Der Führerstaat: Nationalsozialistische Herrschaft, 1933–1945* (The Führer state: National Socialist rule, 1933– 1945) (Munich, 1987), 191.

30. "Die Leibeserziehung in den Hochschulen für Lehrerbildung" (Physical education in teachers' colleges), *Deutsche Volkserziehung* (Education of the German people), no. 1/2 (1937):25.

31. Cited in *Documente der deutschen Politik* (German policy documents), ed. Paul Meyer-Benneckenstein (Berlin, 1933), 1:300– 311.

32. Quoted in Gamm, *Führung und Verführung*, 100.

33. *Hans Schemm spricht: Seine Reden und sein Werk* (Hans Schemm speaks: His speeches and his work), ed. G. Kahl-Furthmann (Bayreuth, 1942), 108ff.

34. *Hans Schemm spricht zur Jugend* (Hans Schemm speaks to young people), ed. G. Kahl-Furthmann (Berlin, 1936), 29.

35. Quoted in Carl Christoph Lingelbach, "Erziehung und Erziehungstheorien im nationalsozialistischen Deutschland" (Education and educational theories in National Socialist Germany) (Ph.D. diss., University of Marburg, 1969), 84, 86.

36. Joseph Goebbels, "Mein Führer!" reprinted in Peter Longerich, *Joseph Goebbels und der totale Krieg: Eine unbekannte Denkschrift des Propagandaministeriums vom 18. Juli 1944*

(Joseph Goebbels and total war: An unknown memorandum from the propaganda minister from 18 July 1944) (Stuttgart, 1987), 20f.

37. *Deutschland Berichte* (Reports from Germany) (1936), 1329.

38. See the essay by Udo R. Rischer, "Die Gefahr der Verweichlichung" (The danger of getting soft), in *Neues Volk: Blätter des rassenpolitischen Amtes* (New People: Papers from the Race Policy Department [of the National Socialist Party]) (December 1933), which addresses those parents who try to keep their children from all that is "hard, rough, and unpleasant." Rischer says that the products of this kind of education will turn into "emasculated weaklings," who "don't know what the word battle means" (29).

39. "Wir sind des Führers Jugend, geeint in seinem Geist. / Wir wollen ewig kämpfen für das, was Deutschland heisst" (*Kinderlandverschickung 1934: NSV Gau Hessen-Nassau* [n.p., 1934], 3).

40. "Blonde und braune Buben / passen nicht in die Stuben. / Buben, die müssen sich schlagen, / müssen was Tollkühnes wagen. / Buben gehören ins Leben hinein; / Buben sind stolz, ob sie gross oder klein. / Trommeln und Pfeifen und Tuben, / das ist der Sang der Buben. / Buben, die trotzten verwegen / Sturmwind, Wetter und Regen. / Buben, die sind von herrischer Art, / Sturmvogel gleich ihre fröhliche Fahrt" (ibid., 1f.).

41. See Kammer and Bartsch, *Jugendlexikon*, 91.

42. Melita Maschmann writes about this perceptively: "It was part of the methodology of the National Socialist youth leadership to carry almost all of this out in the form of competitions. They fought for the highest achievement, not only in sports and in careers. Every unit wanted to have the most beautiful home, the most interesting trip book, to collect the most contributions. Even before the war this constant fight for achievement introduced an element of unrest and forced activity into the life of the groups. It not only picked up on the youthful urge to be active, but it fanned it." See Melita Maschmann, *Fazit—Mein Weg in der Hitler-Jugend* (Taking stock—my life in the Hitler Youth) (Munich, 1980), 183.

43. Klönne, *Jugend im Dritten Reich*, 130.

44. Baldur von Schirach quoted in *Deutsche Zeitung*, 13 January 1934.

45. Quoted in Martin Klaus, *Mädchen in der Hitler-Jugend* (Girls in the Hitler Youth) (Cologne, 1980), 185, 198.

46. Griesmayr and Würschinger, *Idee und Gestalt*, 259. The first air raid on Berlin, which killed eight and wounded twenty-eight, occurred on 29 August 1940.

47. Cf. Heinrich Wollrabenstein, "Die Erweiterte Kinderland-verschickung," *Deutsche Schülererziehung, 1941/42* (Education of German students, 1941/42), 6:93ff.; Harald Scholz, *National-sozialistische Ausleseschulen: Internatschulen als Herrschaftsmittel des Führerstaats* (The elite National Socialist schools: Boarding schools as a means to power in the Hitler regime) (Göttingen, 1973), 285; and Klönne, *Jugend im Dritten Reich*, 55. In a "highly confidential" memorandum dated 27 September 1940, Reichs-leiter Martin Bormann writes with reference to the "Extended KLV": "The Führer has ordered that young people living in areas that are subjected to repeated nighttime air raids be sent, on a voluntary basis, to other areas of the Reich. They are to be put up, keeping their schools and classes intact as far as possible. . . . The following districts are suitable for receiving children from large cities: Bayrische Ostmark, Mark Brandenburg, Ober-donau, Saxony, Silesia, Sudetenland, Wartheland, Ostland" (quoted in Dabel, *KLV*, 7).

48. Baldur von Schirach, *Die Hitler-Jugend: Idee und Gestalt* (Berlin, 1934), 86, 107, 130, 175.

49. See Dienststelle Reichsleiter von Schirach, ed., *Erweiterte Kinderlandverschickung: Anweisungen für die Jungen- und Mädel-lager* (Extended KLV: Instructions for boys' and girls' camps), 2d ed. (Berlin, 1941), 6f.

50. Griesmayr and Würschinger, *Idee und Gestalt*, 260, 263.

51. Rüdiger, *Die Hitler-Jugend*, 292.

52. Griesmayr and Würschinger, *Idee und Gestalt*, 264. The periodical *Das junge Deutschland* (Young Germany) wrote in 1943 that "KLV camps" were now finally equipped "to completely educate young people on a large scale and for an extend-ed period" (103).

53. With regard to the *Selbstführung der Jugend* (Self-guidance of youth), see Günter Kaufmann, *Das kommende Deutschland: Die*

Erziehung der Jugend im Reich Adolf Hitlers (The future Germany: Education of youth in Adolf Hitler's Reich) (Berlin, 1940), 215ff. Also Rüdiger, *Die Hitler-Jugend*, 291, and Scholz, *Nationalsozialistische Ausleseschulen*, 284ff.

54. The program for the monthly political instruction appeared in the periodical *Unser Lager: Richtblätter für die Dienstgestaltung in den Lagern der KLV* (Our camp: Pages laying out the assignment of duties in KLV camps) (Berlin, 1941).

55. See "Ein Hitlerjunge in der Kinderlandverschickung" (A Hitler Youth in the KLV), in *Hitler Jugend: Jugend im Dritten Reich* (Hitler Youth: Youth in the Third Reich), ed. Hermann Glaser and Axel Silenius (Frankfurt am Main, 1975), 59: "Certainly the Lamafüs had a considerably stronger influence than the teachers. Like us, the teachers scarcely dared to say anything because they themselves were subject to censorship by these Lamafüs. In addition, one had the feeling that one was quite helpless, without rights and at their mercy."

56. Indeed, the wrangling over power within the KLV camps reflected the emphasis on competition characteristic of all National Socialist organizations. See Karl Dietrich Bracher, Manfred Funke, and Hans-Adolf Jacobsen, eds., *Nationalsozialistische Diktatur, 1933–1945: Eine Bilanz* (The National Socialist dictatorship, 1933–1945: Taking stock) (Düsseldorf, 1983), 73ff.; and Werner Maser, *Das Regime: Alltag in Deutschland, 1933–1945* (The regime: Everyday life in Germany, 1933–1945) (Munich, 1985), 318f.

57. One of the few exceptions in this regard is Alfred Ehrentreich (*50 Jahre erlebte Schulreform*, 148–75). Although in reporting on his activity as KLV Camp Director in the Sudetenland, he specifically emphasizes that he was not a "PG" (a Party member), he praises Gerhard Dabel (cf. note 4 above) for having put together the "most reliable material describing the KLV" (148), and claims on top of that that the majority of the children who were evacuated still look back on their "KLV time as one of the most powerful experiences" (157).

58. Quoted by Larass, *Der Zug der Kinder*, 204.

59. In an interesting study, Bernhard Haupert and Franz Josef Schäfer pick up some of the issues raised by this question. See *Jugend zwischen Kreuz und Hakenkreuz: Biographische Rekon-*

struktion als Alltagsgeschichte des Nationalsozialismus (Young people between the Cross and the Swastika: Biographical reconstruction of the history of everyday life in National Socialism)
(Frankfurt am Main, 1991). Their method "combines oral history with the technique of social biography and objective her-
meneutics" (9). However, their subject is a boy born in 1924 in
the Saar who grows up in a strict Catholic environment and
becomes a committed Hitler Youth and later a soldier fighting at
the front without having been influenced by the KLV camps.

60. See Roy Pascal, *Die Autobiographie: Gehalt und Gestalt*
(Autobiography: Contents and form) (Stuttgart, 1965), 28ff.

61. See, e.g., Helmut Peitsch, *Deutschlands Gedächtnis an seine
dunkelste Zeit: Zur Funktion der Autobiographik in den Westzonen
Deutschlands und den Westsektoren von Berlin, 1945 bis 1949* (Germany's memory of its darkest period: The function of autobiography in the western zones of Germany and the western sectors
of Berlin, 1945 to 1949) (Berlin, 1990), 9ff.

62. Heinrich Böll quoted in *Materialienbuch Christa Wolf* (Darmstadt-Neuwied, 1979), 8.

AFTER THE FIRST AIR RAIDS
KLV Camp Kirchenpopowc in the Warthegau

1. The term *Pimpf* used to have a disparaging connotation, but
as early as 1900 it was being used in a positive sense by the German *Wandervogel* movement.

2. "Jungvolkjungen sind hart, / schweigsam und treu, / Jungvolkjungen sind Kameraden. / Des Jungvolkjungen Höchstes ist
die Ehre." For more about admission rituals in the Hitler Youth,
see Günter Kaufmann, *Das kommende Deutschland* (Berlin, 1940),
46ff.

3. Jutta Rüdiger, ed., *Die Hitler-Jugend* (Lindhorst, 1983), 27.

4. On this subject, cf. Gerhard Dabel, *KLV* (Freiburg, 1981),
7f., 12.

5. Altogether only 50,000 children were sent into what had
been Poland, mostly to the southern part, especially to Zakopane
and Bad Rabka in the Beskid Mountains. On the other hand,
there were relatively few KLV camps in what had been the
province of Posen, which was called Reichsgau Wartheland after

1939, since this district was intended to receive ethnic Germans from the Baltic areas and Russia. Cf. ibid., 257.

6. Cf. Hans Jakob Schmitz, *Geschichte des Netze-Warthelandes* (The history of the Noteć and Warta Land) (Leipzig, 1941), 308.

7. To keep parents from visiting their children in the KLV camps, the Party leadership sent them regular newsletters that put their children's situation in a better light. A few of these monthly leaflets—like *Die Brücke: Elternbrief der Erweiterten Kinderlandverschickung im Generalgouvernement; Tauerngold: Elternbrief der Erweiterten Kinderlandverschickung, Gau Salzburg; Die Prager Burg: Elternbrief der Erweiterten Kinderlandverschickung in Böhmen und Mähren; Die Brücke im Norden: Elternbrief der Erweiterten Kinderlandverschickung in Dänemark; Nibelungenland: Elternbrief der Erweiterten Kinderlandverschickung, Gau Niederdonau; Das grüne Herz: Elternbrief der Erweiterten Kinderlandverschickung, Gau Thüringen;* and *Elternbrief der Erweiterten Kinderlandverschickung, Gau Nordmark*—are on file in the Koblenz Bundesarchiv (Call no.: ZGs 140). In addition to poems, photographs, amusing stories, letters, and reports about the superior medical care and the good food in the camps, they also contained repeated warnings not to write to the children about the war or the air raids and not to come to the camps to take them back under any circumstances; this would be equal to a "breach of trust toward the Party" (*Elternbrief der Erweiterten Kinderlandverschickung, Gau Nordmark*, February 1941, 9). Visits were also strongly discouraged in the regularly printed "Rules for the Kinderlandverschickung," since it was supposedly "very uncomfortable for a Pimpf" to suddenly be seen as a "'mama's boy' in front of all the other boys." "A brave Pimpf needs to have a brave mother, who can 'hold back' her longing" (ibid., April 1941, 9). Some of these *Elternbriefe* even published the verses of bedazzled Nazi mothers who present the KLV as the "noblest act" of a Führer worried about his people. Here is just one example from the June 1943 issue of *Die Brücke*, submitted by Johanna Binkmann from Cuxhaven: "Ihr Kinderlein, ihr habt es gut / Bei uns im Dritten Reich. / Der Führer nahm Euch treu in Hut, / Ist gleich, ob arm, ob reich. / Er schickte zur Erholung hin / Euch wo es hübsch und fein. / Drum kommt es mir nicht aus dem Sinn, / Ihr müsst ihm dankbar sein! / Ihm Treue halten immerdar / So lang ihr lebt

auf Erden, / Dann wird der Führer doch fürwahr / Mal wieder glücklich werden. / Er liebt sehr unser Vaterland, / Liebt Mann und Frau und Kind. / Erhebet freudig drum die Hand; / 'Heil Hitler!' grüsst geschwind" (Children, you're well off in the Third Reich. Our Führer took you under his wing, both rich and poor. He sent you on vacation to a lovely place. So I keep thinking, you must be grateful to him. You must always be loyal to him as long as you live. Then the Führer will truly be happy again. He loves our Fatherland so very much. Loves man, woman, and child. So, joyfully raise your arm, and quickly greet him with "Heil Hitler") (8).

8. Warme Stuben
    und Zigaretten,
    Goldene Reifen,
    gestärkte Manschetten,
    parfümierte Seifen
    und süsse Buben
    mit Wachsgesicht,
    die wollen wir nicht!

    Wir sind Pimpfe
    mit wilden Mähnen
    und harten Fäusten,
    mit Nagelschuhen
    und lachenden Zähnen,
    die etwas leisten,
    und nimmer ruhen.
    Ob arm oder reich,
    wir sind alle gleich.

Alfred Weidenmann, *Jungzug 2: Fünfzig Jungen im Dienst* (Boys' Platoon No. 2: Fifty boys serving [their country]) (Stuttgart, 1936), 5.

9. Kaufmann, *Das kommende Deutschland*, 91.

10. Weidenmann, *Jungzug 2*, 224.

11. Ibid., 186f. A similar bellicosity prevails in the Hitler Youth novels by Gerhard Dabel, Horst Axmann, and above all in Reinhold Sautler's *Pimpf jetzt gilt's: Das Erlebnis der Jungbann-Fehden* (Pimpf, you're on: The squad feud experience) (1936).

12. Cf. my essay "Frühe musikalische Erlebnisse" (Early mu-

sical experiences), in *Gedenkschrift für Helmut Hopf*, ed. Brunhilde Sonntag (Münster, 1992), 295–302.

THE FÜHRER'S ACT OF GENEROSITY
The KLV Camp in San Remo, Italy

1. What was once identified as tuberculosis of the larynx, we now know to have been throat cancer. [Trans.]

2. Cf. the section "Die Jugendfilmstunden der Hitler-Jugend" (Young people's movie hours in the Hitler Youth), in Hilmar Hoffmann's *"Und die Fahne führt uns in die Ewigkeit": Propaganda im Nationalsozialistischen Film* ("And the flag will lead us into eternity": Propaganda in National Socialist films) (Frankfurt am Main, 1988) 1:100–110.

3. On the subject of "Nordic heroes" as models for "heroic eagerness to fight" in National Socialist education, cf. Peter Aley, *Jugendliteratur im Dritten Reich* (Young people's literature in the Third Reich) (Frankfurt am Main, 1967), 107ff.

4. Cf. Ludwig Schütz, *Schüler-Soldaten: Die Geschichte der Luftwaffenhelfer im Zweiten Weltkrieg* (Young students as soldiers: The story of the Luftwaffe Helpers in the Second World War) (Frankfurt am Main, 1972).

5. On the subject of the Hitler Youth patrols, cf. Jutta Rüdiger, ed. *Die Hitler-Jugend* (Lindhorst, 1983), 63f.; and Karl Heinz Jahnke and Michael Buddrus, eds., *Deutsche Jugend, 1933–1945: Eine Dokumentation* (German youth, 1933–1945: A documentation) (Hamburg, 1989), 311ff.

6. Günter Grass, *Katz und Maus* (Reinbek, 1961), 32. English edition published by Harcourt Brace under the title *Cat and Mouse* (New York, 1963).

7. Cf. Gerhard Dabel, *KLV* (Freiburg, 1981), 20.

THE RENEWED EVACUATION OF MOST CITY CHILDREN
KLV Camp Gross-Ottingen in the Warthegau

1. On the subject of the strict isolation of the KLV camps from the local Polish, Latvian, and Danish populations, see Claus Larass, *Der Zug der Kinder* (Munich, 1983), 109.

2. With regard to the general censoring of letters, cf. ibid., 95.

Even the diaries written by camp participants were censored by the camp squad leaders. One KLV participant later wrote, "You will find many comments in them that certain things were thought of as very snappy (*zackig*) and tough (*stramm*) and wild (*wüst*)—these were popular adjectives in those days." Cf. "Ein Hitler-Junge in der Kinderlandverschickung," in Hermann Glaser and Axel Silenius, eds., *Hitler Jugend* (Frankfurt am Main, 1975), 57.

3. Henry Picker, *Hitlers Tischgespräche* (Munich, n.d.), 63, 107, 119.

4. This contradicts Claus Larass's proposition that Schirach had not succeeded in "eliminating the influence of teachers in the camps" (Larass, *Der Zug der Kinder*, 47, 217).

5. Cf. the documents reproduced in Gerhard Dabel, *KLV* (Freiburg, 1981), 126ff.; Glaser and Silenius, *Hitler Jugend*, 64f.; and Sigrid Bremer, *Muckefuck und Kameradschaft: Mädchenzeit im Dritten Reich, von der Kinderlandverschickung 1940 bis zum Studium 1946* (Ersatz coffee and comradeship: Girlhood in the Third Reich, from KLV 1940 to university 1946), 3d ed. (Frankfurt am Main, 1989), 13ff.

6. At such flag-raisings in other camps there was often a memorial ceremony for Hitler Youths who had been killed in fighting the Communists in the late twenties. Cf. Arno Klönne, *Jugend im Dritten Reich* (Munich, 1980), 58.

7. In Gross-Ottingen we did not get to read monthly KLV magazines like *Junge Heimat* (Young homeland) or other instructional material for study groups and camp instructional evenings that Gerhard Dabel mentions (Dabel, *KLV*, 154ff.).

8. Cf. Martin Wähler, "Das politische Kampflied der Gegenwart" (The political fighting song of today), *Zeitschrift für Deutschkunde* 48 (1934): 137–39. Cf. also Günter Hartung, *Literatur und Ästhetik des deutschen Faschismus* (Literature and aesthetics of German fascism) (Cologne, 1984), 196ff. In particular, Harting points to the significance of Ernst Krieck in the context of fascist musical culture. Krieck, in his book *Musische Erziehung* (Fine arts education) (1933), had presented music as a realm where "discipline" (*Zucht und Ordnung*) operates and the individual submits to the "mysterious primal power of rhythm" (*geheim-*

nisvollen Urgewalt des Rhythmus), which is where "fighting fitness" is achieved "in the spiritual, in attitude, and in ethos" (1).

9. Cf. also Hans-Jochen Gamm, *Der braune Kult* (The Brown cult) (Hamburg, 1962), 16ff.; Glaser and Silenius, *Hitler Jugend*, 51ff.; and Klönne, *Jugend im Dritten Reich*, 65ff.

10. Cf. Baldur von Schirach, ed., *Blut und Ehre: Lieder der Hitlerjugend* (Blood and honor: Songs of the Hitler Youth) (Berlin, 1933), 121f.

11. This song has its origins in an old folksong and had previously been revised by the German Communist Party for its own use. Cf. Ernst Klusen, ed., *Deutsche Lieder* (German songs) (Frankfurt am Main, 1980), 545.

12. My essay "Deutsche fressen Deutsche: Heiner Müllers 'Die Schlacht' an der Ostberliner Volksbühne" (Germans devour Germans: Heiner Müller's "The Battle" performed by East Berlin's Volksbühne) grew out of conversations I had with Müller after the performance about various aspects of National Socialism. See *Brecht-Jahrbuch* (1978), 129–43.

13. Cited in Erika Mann, *Zehn Millionen Kinder: Erziehung der Jugend im Dritten Reich* (Ten million children: Education of young people in the Third Reich) (Munich, 1989), 150.

14. Cf. Max Momsen, "Die Leibeserziehung in den Hochschulen für Lehrerbildung" (Physical training in teachers' colleges), *Deutsche Volkserziehung*, no. 1/2 (1937): 25. Also cf. Paul H. Kuntze, *Entgiftete Brunnen: Zerfall, Abwehr und Gesundung der Nation* (Decontaminated wells: Decay, defense, and healing of the nation) (Munich, 1936), in which the "heroic nature" instilled in "a hard school" is backed up with citations from Nietzsche (101).

15. Cf. Geert Platner, ed., *Schule im Dritten Reich* (Schools in the Third Reich) (Munich, 1983), 21.

16. Cf. Heinrich Kranz, ed., *Der Nationalsozialismus als pädagogisches Problem: Deutsche Erziehungsgeschichte, 1933–1945* (National Socialism as a pedagogical problem: The history of German education, 1933–1945) (Frankfurt am Main, 1984), 133ff.

17. Cf. Paul Seelhoff, *Schule und Nation* (School and nation) (Dortmund, [1935?]), 379ff.

18. Cf. Ernst Bloch, *Freiheit und Ordnung: Abriss der Sozialu-*

topien (Freedom and order: Survey of social utopias) (New York, 1946).

19. Bertolt Brecht, *Gesammelte Werke in acht Bänden* (Collected works in eight volumes) (Frankfurt am Main, 1967), 4:434.

20. Cf. Wolfgang Fritz Haug, *Die Faschisierung des bürgerlichen Subjekts* (The fascization of the middle-class subject) (Berlin, 1986), 92.

21. Cf. Hermann Giesecke, "Die Hitlerjugend," in *Die Formung des Volksgenossen: Der "Erziehungsstaat" des Dritten Reiches* (The shaping of the national comrade: The "educational state" of the Third Reich), ed. Ulrich Herrmann (Weinheim, 1985), 180.

22. Cited in Wolfgang Promies, ed., *Erziehung zum Krieg—Krieg als Erzieher: Mit dem Jugendbuch für Kaiser, Vaterland und Führer* (Education for war—war as educator: With children's books for Kaiser, Fatherland, and Führer) (Oldenburg, 1979), 58.

23. Cf. Harald Scholz, *Erziehung und Unterricht unterm Hakenkreuz* (Education and instruction under the Swastika) (Göttingen, 1985), 120; and Manfred Behrens et al., eds., *Faschismus und Ideologie* (Fascism and ideology), (Berlin, 1980), 1:162f.

24. Picker, *Hitlers Tischgespräche*, 97f., 366.

25. Many National Socialists operated on the basis of theories about "physical training of the German people" spelled out in Hitler's *Mein Kampf:* "The school in a volkish state must make much more time available for physical training. Not a day must go by on which the young person is not given one hour of physical training, both in the morning and in the evening, and that should be in all sorts of sports and gymnastics." Cited in Hasso von Wedel, *Wehrerziehung und Volkserziehung* (Military training and Volk education) (Hamburg, 1938), 38.

26. Cf. Martin Broszat, *Nationalsozialistische Polenpolitik* (National Socialist policy for Poland) (Stuttgart, 1961); Martin Broszat, *Zweihundert Jahre deutsche Polenpolitik* (Two hundred years of German Poland policy) (Frankfurt am Main, 1972); and Czeslaw Madajczyk, *Die Okkupationspolitik Nazideutschlands in Polen, 1939–1945* (The occupation policy of Nazi Germany in Poland, 1939–1945) (Berlin, 1987).

27. Cf. in general my chapter "Hopes for a Greater German

Reich in the East," in *Old Dreams of a New Reich: Volkish Utopias and National Socialism* (Bloomington, 1992); as well as Robert L. Koehl, *RWFDV: German Resettlement and Population Policy, 1939–1945: A History of the Reich Commission for the Strengthening of Germandom* (Cambridge, 1957); and the key words *Eindeutschung*, *Germanisierung*, and *Volksdeutsche*, in Hilde Kammer and Elisabet Bartsch, eds., *Jugendlexikon Nationalsozialismus* (Reinbek, 1990), 53–55, 77f., 219–21. As early as 28 November 1939, Reinhard Heydrich was given the assignment to "clear the new eastern territories of Jews and Poles." Cited in Broszat, *Nationalsozialistische Polenpolitik*, 85. Hitler saw the population groups to be "cleansed" contemptuously as "Jews, Polacks, and other riffraff" (ibid., 25).

28. Cf. Arthur Greiser, *Der Aufbau im Osten* (Building up in the east) (Jena, 1942).

29. Picker, *Hitlers Tischgespräche*, 285, 287, 294. Hitler did not even shy away from voicing such opinions in public. Thus he declared in a Reichstag speech on 6 October 1939 that this "ridiculous Polish state," this "pet of the Western democracies," was never really a viable state, and therefore had to be "swept from the surface of the earth." Cited in Broszat, *Zweihundert Jahre*, 277.

30. Cf. Christoph Klessmann, "Die Zerstörung des Schulwesens als Bestandteil deutscher Okkupationspolitik im Osten am Beispiel Polen" (The destruction of schools as a component of German occupation policy in the east taking Poland as an example), in *Erziehung und Schulung im Dritten Reich* (Education and indoctrination in the Third Reich), ed. Manfred Heinemann (Stuttgart, 1980), 1:176ff.

31. Cf. Hans-Hochen Gamm, *Führung und Verführung* (Munich, 1964), 449.

32. Ibid., 440ff.; and Kranz, *Nationalsozialismus als pädagogisches Problem*, 284ff.

33. *Lebensborn* was an SS organization that provided safe homes for mothers of progeny sired by SS men and other "racially valuable" Germans. [Trans.] Cf. Gamm, *Führung und Verführung*, 453.

34. About so-called courts martial as well as other terrorist

acts of the SS in the Warthegau, cf. Broszat, *Nationalsozialistische Polenpolitik*, 119ff. Heinrich Himmler did not stop taking such measures even when Arthur Greiser protested (ibid., 153). The Racial Policy Office of the Nazi Party in Berlin reacted similarly; in 1942 it declared in a brochure titled *Nationalsozialistische Fremdvolkpolitik* (National Socialist policy toward foreigners): "The long-term goal of a foreign policy oriented along racial lines can only be the removal of the majority of Poles from the Reich" (cited in ibid., 278).

35. Gerhard Dabel's book *Rurik: Geschichtliche Erzählung* (Rurik: A historical tale) (Leipzig, 1943), appeared as volume 9 in the "Lagerbücherei der Kinderlandverschickung" series. The story underscores Dabel's support for the fascist eastern policy in the framework of KLV management. Rurik is described as the "most important leader personality" among the Danish-Saxon Varangians. As the first "Nordic hero," he attempts in his advance eastward to "organize" the "huge area between Europe and Asia" politically, and this process is indirectly presented as a precursor to Hitler's Germanization policy with regard to Poland and Russia (223). Moreover, since 1936 Dabel had been a frequent winner of awards for his National Socialist books for young people. Cf. Peter Aley, *Jugendliteratur im Dritten Reich* (Frankfurt am Main, 1967), 72ff.

36. Cited in Larass, *Der Zug der Kinder*, 56. Even Gerhard Dabel admits that in some camps there were cases where boys took the law into their own hands, but he blames these cases largely on "uncomradely behavior" or "stealing from comrades" (*KLV*, 131).

37. Günter de Bruyn described similar scenes in his autobiographical *Zwischenbilanz* (Frankfurt am Main, 1992). "Some weak boy," he writes in connection with a description of his KLV experiences in the year 1940, "would be pulled out of bed by masked boys on the pretense that he would miss washing himself or that he was telling tales or behaving effeminately. They would work him over with scrubbing brushes in the washroom, pour cold water over him, and beat him. Once this happened to a boy from our room, and instead of helping him, the rest of us pretended we were asleep in the hope that we'd be spared" (111).

1. These camps in which Hitler Youths were supposed to receive premilitary training can be traced back to an order issued by Hitler in October 1939. The department responsible for military training in the Office of the Reich Youth Leader (*Reichsjugendführer*) was the Office for Physical Training (*Amt für körperliche Ertüchtigung*) Cf. Hilde Kammer and Elisabet Bartsch, *Jugendlexikon Nationalsozialismus* (Reinbek, 1990), 232f. The Wehrmacht and the SS had been vying since 1940 for control over these premilitary camps, a struggle in which Reich Youth Leader Artur Axmann sided with the SS. See documents in Karl Heinz Jahnke and Michael Buddrus, eds., *Deutsche Jugend* (Hamburg, 1989), 165f., 318–20, 327–33, 352, 357f. In addition to the camps like ours that were under SS control, there were therefore also camps where the army or the air force was in control and in which fourteen-to-sixteen-year-old Hitler Youths were trained in shooting small-bore rifles, glider flying, or service as field medics, and so on.

2. Even though the Waffen-SS comprised only 3 percent of the total strength of the German army, their trainers were in charge of more than 25 percent of all the premilitary training camps. About 90,000 Hitler Youths went through their forty-two camps annually between 1942 and 1944. See Jahnke and Buddrus, *Deutsche Jugend*, 357f.

3. Ibid., 365.

4. Reprinted in ibid., 372.

EPIDEMICS AND THE FIRST PROTESTS
KLV Camp Gross-Ottingen in the Warthegau

1. Cf. Hasso von Wedel, *Wehrerziehung und Volkserziehung* (Military training and Volk education) (Hamburg, 1938), 64.

2. Cf. Karl Heinz Jahnke and Michael Buddrus, eds., *Deutsche Jugend* (Hamburg, 1989), 365.

3. Cf. Henry Picker, *Hitlers Tischgespräche* (Munich, n.d.), 73ff., 80ff.

4. Claus Larass even quotes an inspection report which said: "Twenty-two girls live in the camp. They all have lice. Dorle H.'s infestation has reached a stage I have never seen before. Her neck and ears are chewed up. Eight girls also have scabies. One sick child was in bed for ten days without any care." See Claus Larass, *Der Zug der Kinder* (Munich, 1983), 97.

5. See, e.g., George Fischer, *Soviet Opposition to Stalin: A World War II Case Study* (Cambridge, 1952), 72–83; and Wilfried Strik-Strikfeld, *Gegen Stalin und Hitler: General Wlassow und die russische Freiheitsbewegung* (Opposing Stalin and Hitler: General Wlassow and the Russian freedom movement) (Frankfurt am Main, 1970).

THE LAST STAND
KLV Camp Sulmierschütz in the Warthegau

1. Cited in Karl Heinz Jahnke and Michael Buddrus, eds., *Deutsche Jugend* (Hamburg, 1989), 388f.

2. *NSV-Schweinchen* (little NSV pig) was the common term for the notice board shaped like a little pig that hung in every house and on which were listed what sort of kitchen scraps a pig will eat. Hilde Kammer and Elisabet Bartsch, *Jugendlexikon National-sozialismus* (Reinbek, 1990), 145. Kammer and Bartsch also write, "A housewife's insufficient willingness to collect scraps often led to denunciation by her block warden."

3. Cf. Martin Broszat, *Zweihundert Jahre deutsche Polenpolitik* (Frankfurt am Main, 1972), 286ff.

4. Similar things are reported by Gerhard Dabel, *KLV* (Freiburg, 1981), 120; and Claus Larass, *Der Zug der Kinder* (Munich, 1983), 68.

RETURN AND READJUSTMENT
Rauischholzhausen and Kassel

1. Two workers I met in a Rauischholzhausen country inn in 1988 gave me this information; they were very proud of their Mr. Kaiser.

2. My paternal grandfather was an American citizen and had held on to his citizenship even after he moved back to Germany.

Therefore, when my father was born in Kassel in 1905, he was an "American."

3. Some researchers into fascism referring to this syndrome speak of "posthypnotic determination." See Harald Scholz, *Nationalsozialistiche Ausleseschulen* (Göttingen, 1973), 387.

4. Cf. Peter Sloterdijk, *Literatur und Organisation von Lebenserfahrung: Autobiographien der zwanziger Jahre* (Literature and organization of experiences: Autobiographies of the twenties) (Munich, 1978), 13.

5. Perhaps the fact that Franz Kaiser was not only a farmer, but also a politician, writer, and researcher into local history may have contributed to this. See, e.g. , his contributions in the periodical *Gestern und Heute: Marburger und Biedenkopfer Land*, no. 1 (1978): 7f., 18–26; as well as his essay in the brochure *1200 Jahre Rauischholzhausen: Festschrift aus Anlass der 1200-Jahrfeier des Ortsteils Rauischholzhausen der Gemeinde Ebsdorfer Grund* (Twelve hundred years of Rauischholzhausen: Festschrift on the occasion of the 1200th anniversary of Rauischholzhausen, community of Ebsdorfer Grund) (Marburg, 1981), 15f.

6. See Jost Hermand, *Kultur im Wiederaufbau: Die Bundesrepublik Deutschland, 1945–1965* (Culture in reconstruction: The Federal Republic of Germany, 1945–1965) (Munich, 1986), 272ff.

7. See my essay "Neuordnung oder Restauration? Zur Beurteilung der faschistischen Kunstdiktatur in der unmittelbaren Nachkriegszeit" (A new order or restoration? Judging the fascist dictatorship in the arts during the postwar period), in *Kritische Berichte* 12, no. 1 (1984): 78–83; and no. 2 (1984): 69–79.

8. These disillusionments probably found their "darkest" expression in a play I wrote during the winter of 1948–49. Called *Sisyphos* (Sisyphus), it was based on Albert Camus's book *Der Mythos vom Sisyphos* (The myth of Sisyphus). The play was intended as a "multimedia" work of total nihilism, depicting— with actors, black backdrops, a chorus, and piano music that I had composed—the great boulder rolling downward and the helpless rage of the protagonist. I began rehearsals for the piece in the summer of 1949 with a group of classmates and women graduates from the Heinrich Schütz School; I hoped to present the drama as part of the graduation ceremony in our makeshift school auditorium. When the director of the school got wind of

this, he immediately demanded to see the script of my *Sisyphos;* three days later he told me that unfortunately he would have to forbid me from performing this piece. One could not confront the parents who were attending the graduation ceremony and were justifiably proud of their sons with such a nihilistic play, he said. And so, when the diplomas were handed out, a modern string quartet was performed, which didn't say anything to anyone, but neither did it offend any ideological sensibilities.

9. See Hermand, *Kulture im Wiederaufbau,* 251ff.

10. Wolfgang Abendroth told me in a personal conversation that his first lecture in Marburg was attended by only seven students. Later he wrote: "The student body in Marburg during this time was dominated by fraternities; practically no oppositional thought existed." See Wolfgang Abendroth, *Ein Leben in der Arbeiterbewegung* (A life in the labor movement), ed. Barbara Dietrich and Joachim Perels (Frankfurt am Main, 1976), 217.

11. Reinhard Kühnl, *Formen bürgerlicher Herrschaft: Liberalismus—Faschismus* (Forms of middle-class power: Liberalism–fascism) (Reinbek, 1971).

EPILOGUE
A Journey into the Past

1. However, many weeks later I received a letter from the school administration in which they at least gave me the first names of my former teachers.

2. In addition to the documents bequeathed to it by the Freiburg KLV Arbeitsgemeinschaft (The KLV Study Group), the Federal Archive in Koblenz also has the National Socialist propaganda film *Hände hoch!* (Put your hands up!) (1942). This film depicts the camp life of children evacuated to Czechoslovakia, and includes as well all fourteen of the National Socialist newsreels that deal with the KLV. See Peter Bucher, ed., *Wochenschauen und Dokumentarfilme* (Koblenz, 1984); *Stichwort "Kinderlandverschickung"* (Keyword "Kinderlandverschickung"); and the catalog of the exhibition, *Jugend im Nationalsozialistischen-Staat* (Young people in the National Socialist state), published by the Bundesarchiv (Koblenz, 1982).

3. Although the Documentation Study Group and Circle of

Friends of the KLV (*Dokumentations-Arbeitsgemeinschaft und Freundeskreis KLV, E.V.*) in Bochum, under the chairmanship of Gustav Post, has no camp documents, it regularly sends out long circulars and maintains a search and job-finding service for former KLV participants. The spirit that prevails in this organization is illustrated by their sixty-first letter dated December 1991. In addition to Christmas greetings, birthday congratulations, news about the Sauerland Mountain Club, and poems about the Danube Swabians and South Tirolians, a "Hymn to the German Language" by Josef Weinheber and information about the Bismarck Medallion being awarded to deserving organization members, there was also an obituary for the Hitler Youth Bannführer, KLV inspector, and SS tank battalion private Walter Lodders. Private Lodders, it says, "did not let them break his back," even in the internment camps after the war, but continued to remain true to his old ideals, for which he was named "Hauptmann der 'Lützower Jäger von 1813'" (Captain of the Lützow Riflemen of 1813) and presented with the Bismarck Silver Medallion in 1990 shortly before his death (57f.).

4. The letter *y* in German is sometimes pronounced like *ü*. [Trans.]

5. See Gottfried Griesmayr and Otto Würschinger, *Idee und Gestalt* (Leonie, 1979). The authors say that the last weeks of the war demonstrated how much the spirit of "readiness to make sacrifices, defiance of death, love of freedom, courage, asceticism, ties to the Volk, and faith in a higher law" prevailed among the Hitler Youth (271).

6. See Karl Heinz Jahnke and Michael Buddrus, eds., *Deutsche Jugend* (Hamburg, 1989), 406ff.

7. I base this on Wilhelm Hehlmann, *Wörterbuch der Psychologie* (Dictionary of psychology) (Stuttgart, 1974), where "repression" is defined as "the process in which ideas, wishes, emotional drives (esp. libidinous ones) are excluded from the conscious without leaving any memory behind. As a result of 'censorship' (superego, conscience, society) they dwell in the area of the 'subconscious' but do not lose their energy. This energy is directed in a changed form into substitute actions, 'symptoms,' Freudian slips, and dreams" (574).

8. Margarete Mitscherlich, *Erinnerungsarbeit: Zur Psycho-*

analyse der Unfähigkeit zu trauern (The work of remembering: On the psychoanalysis of the inability to mourn) (Frankfurt am Main, 1987), 16, 115.